museums and monuments XIX

Titles in this series:

manual on systems
of inventorying
immovable cultural property

Meredith H. Sykes

Unesco

To my parents

1777

PACSYK)

The author is responsible for the choice and the presentation
of the facts contained in this book and for the opinions
expressed therein, which are not necessarily those of Unesco
and do not commit the Organization.

Published in 1984 by the United Nations
Educational, Scientific and Cultural Organization
7 place de Fontenoy, 75700 Paris
Typeset by Text Processing Ltd, Clonmel, Ireland
Printed by Imprimerie de la Manutention, Mayenne

ISBN 92-3-102080-3

We unite all things by perceiving the law which pervades them; by perceiving the superficial differences and the profound resemblances.

Ralph Waldo Emerson

Preface

The inventory is a basic tool for the management of any resource. It is indispensable for the drawing up and implementaton of policy with respect to the preservation and presentation of cultural property. Monuments and sites, museum objects and many other manifestations of our cultural heritage, both tangible and intangible, exist in vast numbers throughout the world. It is only when they are properly listed, identified, and classified that programmes for their protection can be systematically planned and carried through.

Although the process of identifying immovable cultural property has advanced considerably in some countries, in many of the Member States of Unesco inventories are still lacking. In certain cases, the scarcity of human and material resources may have prevented the responsible authorities from launching the inventory process; this has no doubt been due in some measure to the sheer lack of information on simple yet effective methods. In other cases, inventories have been launched but are held up by conceptual and practical difficulties of various kinds. Nevertheless, a variety of successful inventories are now in use in various parts of the world; they reflect different socio-cultural conditions and national tempers and cater to different types of cultural property and conservation needs.

The study and comparison of these varying national situations have been promoted in recent years by Unesco, with the co-operation of the International Council on Monuments and Sites (ICOMOS). These activities were undertaken in accordance with Unesco's Medium Term Plan for 1977–1982 (19C/4 Approved). In September 1977, ICOMOS organized a meeting of inventory specialists in Warsaw, Poland, whose purpose was to analyse the inventory systems used by various countries in Europe and North America. At this meeting, the need for a guide to such existing inventory systems, which would also serve as a manual for creating new systems, was strongly stressed. Further study of the question revealed that such a manual was particularly needed in developing countries, many of whose heritage conservation authorities were already asking themselves which system they could and should adopt.

The idea of preparing the present work was thus taken up. In September 1980, ICOMOS organized, again on behalf of Unesco, a second meeting of experts with the express purpose of determining the nature and contents of the manual. It emerged quite clearly from the discussions that the work would have to describe a significant range of different inventory systems for the benefit of all those who, at national, regional or local levels, wish to adopt or modify an inventory system according to local needs and the resources available. The meeting recommended also that Meredith Sykes be entrusted with the task of preparing the manual, which would consist of methodological introduction based on the analysis and comparison of the inventory systems selected and give detailed information on their methods and functioning.

Soon after the September 1980 meeting ICOMOS created an International Committee on Inventories. The present manual, work on which was completed in 1982, was received and endorsed by this specialized body. It is our hope, therefore, that it will prove to be a useful methodological instrument for specialists and decision-makers throughout the world. We hope also that it will fulfil Unesco's more general aim of gathering and making available internationally professional information of the highest order. Given the scope and level of the work, it is being published in Unesco's long-established series of technical manuals entitled 'Museums and Monuments'.

The author

Born in the State of New Jersey, Meredith Sykes acquired a B.A. in Philosophy at New York University and an M.A. in Art History at Columbia University, where she also attended the graduate programme in historic preservation and lectured on the subject. She is known for her work on two major inventories of immovable cultural properties. As co-designer of the Canadian Inventory of Historic Building she helped develop its pioneering use of illustrated building typologies and computer data management. In 1977 New York City employed her to design and organize the inventory of all 850,000 structures of its built environment. As Director of the city's Urban Cultural Resources Survey she developed techniques which stressed speed of data acquisition and flexible computer-search strategies. These resulted in the recording of 50,000 structures in the first eighteen months of operation. She is a founding member and past president of the Association for Preservation Technology and a member of the ICOMOS International Committee for Inventories. She is currently an independent consultant residing in Paris.

Contents

Contents

Foreword

Listing and classification: it would be hard to find a more universal activity. But while there are only two or three ways of counting (in tens, dozens or pairs, etc.), there are any number of ways of classifying. Classification and identification: ever since Babel the attempt has forced men apart as much as it has drawn them together.

For the last couple of hundred years or so men have been trying, in one place or another, to calculate, identify and clarify the treasures of the mind. For once these lists are not intended to be exhaustive, but to be meaningful, to reveal a hidden sense, they are inventions rather than inventories.

While these efforts are not exactly labours of Sisyphus, they do require a combination of temerity and ingenuousness: characteristics which explain no doubt the great enthusiasm, the occasional solitude and the almost inevitable penury of the men and women who carry them out. In search of their own roots, many of these people turn more readily to historical research than to dialogue with their colleagues in other countries; other colleagues, on the other hand, aspire to such parallel paths of activity. All of them, however, seek to break out of the limits of their scholarly isolation, although this intention does not always manifest itself very clearly.

An International Committee for inventories of immovable cultural property created by the International Council on Monuments and Sites (ICOMOS) proposes to end that isolation and to establish links and exchanges among specialists throughout the world. Its first seeds were sown at a colloquium held in Europe, but the concerns expressed there went beyond the frontiers of this continent.

The present manual by Meredith Sykes will dissipate all idealistic illusions—if any still remain—on the nature of this objective. There can be no question of seeking a unique language, one universal method to inventory so many distinct heritages. The comparison of various inventory systems does not imply the suppression of cultural difference. Rather, as this work does, it should help all those concerned to create their own methods of identifying cultural property and forge the tools needed to analyse it.

In the inventory of its heritage each country has a means to conserve, take possession or resume possession of its cultural indentity. The inventory process seeks out the differences as much as the resemblances, it pinpoints the specificities as much as the mutual and successive influences. The 'dialogue' between inventory systems does not claim, however, to be the indispensable prelude to cultural dialogue. But the one can and must enrich the other.

Meredith Sykes is a pioneer. She has already conceived two inventory systems for the New World and there is little she does not know of the patrimony of the Old. There is no one better placed than she to launch international communication between inventory systems and begin the forging of the tools required. It is my earnest hope that the tools to come will be as finely wrought as this one.

Michel Berthod
Chairman of the ICOMOS
International Committee on Inventories

Introduction

Inventories are an indispensable and fundamental tool for the protection and conservation of the immovable cultural heritage. This manual is conceived for those at national, regional or local levels who have had neither the opportunity nor the funding and personnel to develop and implement their own system for inventorying. A significant range of different methods is described.

The present study is the outcome of a meeting of inventory specialists in Paris, from 15 to 18 September 1980, organized by ICOMOS on behalf of Unesco. The Paris meeting was, itself, a follow-up to an earlier meeting of inventory specialists held in Warsaw three years earlier.

Logic dictated that existing inventory systems be used as the basis for creating a framework of methodology that readers could adopt and modify to their local conditions.

Eleven such systems (listed on page 17) were chosen by the Paris meeting to be representative of different needs and conditions in the world and to demonstrate different technical approaches to surveying common subject-matter, immovable cultural property.

Within this Manual the terms inventory and survey are used interchangeably to mean the organized recording of information. All possess two main features: a methodology and a form. The Manual is organized around the components of these features and is presented in such a way that the reader could adopt, modify or design a system by choosing among the abundant examples drawn fom the eleven systems where the information given seems to parallel the reader's own needs.

The interplay between the components of any survey of cultural properties is basically the following. An 'organization' is established with specific goals to be fulfilled by providing its users with certain products. These products are generally informational in character. The information begins as raw data collected by staff and volunteers on 'forms'. The 'methodology' is the procedure for translating organizational objectives into questions on a form, and thence from raw data to products designed to meet these objectives.

Part One: Overview of methodology

Because methodology is the thread linking system goals with their successful fulfilment, the Manual begins with an overview of this subject which includes: (a) system purpose and objectives; (b) criteria for coverage, selection and legal considerations; (c) users, needs and products; (d) existing resources, staff and volunteers and outside assistance; (e) technical procedures (method) and computerization; and (f) costs and time.

To illustrate these points examples are drawn from the descriptions of the eleven systems and from an analysis of the questions they ask. In order to help focus thinking about these components of system design, a Planning Worksheet (page 135) provides space for the reader to note those aspects that might be relevant to his own needs.

Part Two: System description

The basic data about each of the eleven systems is presented in four sections: (a) a point-by-point discussion of the system's methodology; (b) a summary evaluation; (c) an analysis of all questions from that system's forms which deal with immovable cultural property; (d) an appendix where copies of translated questions are given.[1]

1. Facsimiles of original documents can be found at the end of the Manual.

Information for system descriptions was derived from a questionnaire sent to all system directors who were asked to return it with blank and completed examples of their forms as well as any manuals, lexicons or other descriptive material. Additional correspondence elicited further clarifications where necessary.

Diversity was the first problem to be dealt with: diversity of approach (eleven systems on five continents); diversity of language (six, though two (Japanese and Polish) had been translated); and diversity of forms (twenty-three chosen for the Manual, which record immovable cultural properties and include over 600 questions).

Homogeneity was achieved by first translating all descriptive information and questions into English. Descriptions of the individual systems then were placed in a standardized format. They are also presented in abbreviated form in the System Comparison Chart (page 139). Thus the reader may peruse the individual system description and also compare, point by point, the same methodological features within the other systems. Questions from the individual forms for each system were placed in a thematic and logical framework of seven main categories imposed by the Manual.

Part Three: Question Comparison

The actual questions asked and how they are asked is at the heart of the problem of surveying cultural property. The Outline of Question Categories and Topics introduces this concluding section of the Manual. All questions asked on those forms chosen to be analysed are brought together, topic by topic, in twenty-six Analytic Charts, each followed by Discussion and Recommendations. This permits the reader to compare in one place what questions the various systems ask (or omit) about a given subject.

Two additional graphic aids help the reader further to understand and use this material. A Question Typology Chart summarizes these question types and ranks the importance of their information levels (primary, secondary and optional). Primary questions exact the most basic information and should be necessary to virtually all systems. The Synthesis Grid graphically represents three-dimensionally the distribution of questions by topic/category and survey form/system.

Acknowledgements

This book is based upon the work and assistance of many people. I am sincerely indebted to the directors and individuals associated with the various systems who responded to the letters of query and provided detailed explanations of their respective systems. Many other persons provided general information.

Argentina: Carlos Pernaut, Director, Sistema Automatizado de Inventario y Registro de Monumentos y Sitios, and Jorge Osvaldo Gazaneo.

Canada: B. A. Humphreys, Chief, Canadian Inventory of Historic Building and Robert M. Harrold, Head, Data Collection Systems.

France: Michel Berthod, Sous-Directeur, Inventaire Général des Monuments et des Richesses Artistiques de la France, Marie-Claude Méplan, *chercheur* and J. M. Perouse de Montclos, Maître de Recherches at CNRS, Chargé de Mission d'Inspection Générale at the Inventaire Général.

India: K. M. Srivastava, Director (Monuments), Archaeological Survey of India.

Italy: Oreste Ferrari, Directore, Istituto Centrale per il Catalogo e la Documentazione.

Japan: Nobuto Ito, Director-General, Tokyo National Research Institute of Cultural Properties.

Mexico: Carlos Chanfon-Olmos, Ex-Director, Catalogación Sistema Culhuacán.

Morocco: Abdelhafid El Badmoussi, Chef du Service de la Documentation, Bibliographique, Iconographique et Sonore.

New York City: Kent W. Barwick, Chairman, Landmarks Preservation Commission.

Poland: Wojciech Kalinowski, Director, Historical Monuments Documentation Centre, Marek Konopka, Vice-Director, and Krzystof Palowski, Assistant-Director, Historical Monuments.

Zambia: N. M. Katanekwa, Director, National Monuments Commission and Robin Derricourt, Ex-Director.

ICOMOS: Delphine Lapeyre, Chief of the Documentation Centre.

On a more personal level my concepts of the necessity for, and approaches to, inventory and survey are of course the result of work on two of these systems. To have been one of the original designers of the Canadian Inventory of Historic Building and then to have later designed the Urban Cultural Resources Survey for New York City were both professional privileges and personal pleasures. To the staffs of both the CIHB and UCRS with whom I worked I owe many of the ideas expressed in this book. Last, but not least, I thank William A. Graham for his dedicated assistance and inspiration throughout the writing of the manuscript.

M.H.S.

List of systems analysed

Each of the eleven systems chosen by the Paris working group to represent the various regions and conditions in the world is identified below alphabetically by name of country or area. Full mailing address is given. In order to facilitate reference to the systems and their forms on the Analytic Charts and elsewhere in the Manual, each system is assigned a two-letter country abbreviation or a three-letter city abbreviation. For systems where more than one form has been analysed, each receives its own number. An asterisk (*) denotes that the form is reproduced in full.

Country and identifier	System name, address and forms analysed
Argentina	Sistema Automatizado de Inventario y Registro de Monumentos y Sitios (SIRAMS), Casilla de Correo 4900, 1000 Buenos Aires.
AR1	Monumentos
AR2	Sitios
Canada	Canadian Inventory of Historic Building (CIHB), National Historic Parks and Sites Branch, Parks Canada, Les Terrasses de la Chaudière, Ottawa, Ontario K1A 1G2.
CA*	Recording Form
France	Inventaire Général des Monuments et des Richesses Artistiques de la France (IGRAF), Grand Palais des Champs-Elysées, Porte C, 75008 Paris.
FR*	Bordereau architecture
India	Record of Protected Monuments and Sites, Archaeological Survey of India, Janpath 11, New Delhi.
IN1*	Form A—Record of Protected monuments and Sites
IN2	List of Centrally protected Monuments and Sites

List of systems analysed

Country and identifier	System name, address and forms analysed
Italy	Catalogo dei Beni Culturali, Istituto Centrale per il Catalogo e la Documentazione, Piazza di Porta Portese, 1, 00153 Roma.
IT1*	Scheda A—Architettura
IT2	Scheda SU—Settore Urbano
IT3	Intercalare—Repertorio Indagine Storica
IT4	Intercalare—Repertorio Stato Attuale
Japan	Ledger for Designated Cultural Property, Agency for Cultural Affairs, 3-2-2 Kasumigaseki, Chiyoda-ku, Tokyo 100.
JP1	Ledger of National Treasures and/or Important Cultural Properties
JP2*	Ledger of Historic Sites, Places of Scenic Beauty and/or National Monuments
JP3	Ledger of Important Preservation Districts for Groups of Historic Buildings
Mexico	Catalogación Sistema Culhuacán, Exconvento de Churubusco, General Anaya y 20 de Agosto, Coyoácan, México 21, D.F.
MX1*	Cuestionario No. 1—Monumentos Religiosos
MX2	Monumentos y Lugares de Belleza Natural

Country and identifier	System name, address and forms analysed
Morocco	Inventaire National du Patrimoine Culturel, Ministère d'Etat Chargé des Affaires Culturelles, Rabat.
MA1	Liste Générale des Monuments et Sites
MA2	Site
MA3*	Monument
New York City	Urban Cultural Resources Survey (UCRS), Landmarks Preservation Commission, 20 Vesey Street, New York, NY 10011.
NYC*	UCRS Field Form
Poland	System of Inventorying Historical Monuments, Historical Monuments Documentation Centre, Brzozowa 35, 00-258 Warsawa.
PL1	Address Form
PL2	Historical City or Town Cover Sheet
PL3*	Immovable Historical Monuments Inventory Sheet
Zambia	Zambia National Site Index, National Monuments Commission, P.O. Box 60124, Livingstone.
ZM*	Zambia Site Record Card

Part One

Overview of
methodology

If methodology is a thread linking the intertwining, interacting elements of a survey—its purpose, scope, products, resources, procedures and costs—then we will grasp it by the broad end—purpose—to begin.

1. Purpose and objectives

A cultural heritage survey should define, at its very origins, the fundamental reason for its existence—its basic purpose and objectives—in a statement that is, in effect, the 'guidelines' of the endeavour. This may be intangible and will certainly be unique to each system, reflecting the other tangible considerations that are listed on the Planning Worksheet.

A brief statement of basic purpose is frequently supplemented by secondary and more specific objectives. These may be modified by a time-frame: short range, intermediate or long range. The System Comparison Chart (page 139) succinctly lists the stated purpose and objectives for the eleven systems covered by the Manual and will not be repeated here.

All the systems discussed in the Manual in one way or another record, inventory or identify immovable cultural property. France and Italy both embrace 'research' as a basic purpose. Poland and Italy both include 'collection of documentation'. 'To publicize' is further cited by France.

Besides their basic purposes most systems have additional objectives in which they generally state why or by what means the inventory will be carried out. For example Canada, Morocco, New York City and Poland all include legal designation or protection as an objective. Further specifications may elaborate by what means the work will be done. Italy notes the need to respond to regional resources. Argentina, Canada, Italy and Mexico refer to the kind of system itself (rapid retrieval, computerized, etc.).

> *Worksheet instructions (Purpose and objectives)*
> Define the fundamental reasons why the inventory is desired. List short-range, intermediate and long-range objectives. (See Planning Worksheet, page 135.)

2. Criteria

The Manual considers three types of criteria: general coverage or scope (buildings, archaeology, sites, for example); selection criteria (historic buildings older than 1914); and legal criteria (only such buildings legally designated or protected by the state).

A. COVERAGE

Surveys, in the extreme, can approach their subject-matter in two ways; they are either comprehensive or selective. In terms of the scope of their criteria for the inclusion of cultural properties, many surveys fall between the extremes, or they are comprehensive for some things and selective for others. For example, New York City records all buildings and certain important urban features.

The comprehensive/selective decision may be written into the survey's basic purpose or it may be a reflection of financial and human resource constraints.

The eleven systems analysed here vary greatly in their scope. Their one point in common is coverage of immovable cultural property. Six do only that (Argentina, Canada, India, Mexico, New York City and Zambia). France, Italy and Poland inventory movable properties as well; Japan and Morocco further record cultural intangibles such as human skills.

Actual coverage of the immovable heritage embraces an overlapping range of subjects. The term 'monuments' recurs frequently, though it may have a different meaning for the different systems that use it (Argentina, Mexico, Morocco, Poland). Monuments may be further defined as 'historic' (Poland) or the word can be replaced by more specific terms such as 'architecture' (France and Italy) or 'building' (Canada).

Because some monuments are situated in areas (large or small) with heritage value most systems include terms such as 'site', 'ensemble', 'district', 'urban sector' or 'collective'. Natural sites may also be included.

Many systems also provide for inclusion of other elements related to individual buildings, ensembles or districts such as cemeteries, gardens and parks.

Nearly all the eleven systems also include archaeology within their purview, although such archaeological surveys are not analysed herein unless the same forms primarily used for individual buildings, groups of buildings and districts are used for archaeology as well.

The relation of coverage and forms is worth mentioning. Systems whose coverage is fairly restrictive in scope, though not necessarily in quantity of entries, focus their collection efforts in one form (Canada, New York City and Zambia). The more comprehensive the coverage, however, the greater the number of forms that may be required with consequently a greater effort expended on archiving and cross-referencing this collected data. (Italy's exhaustive approach requires twenty-seven forms plus inserts).

For more details on coverage, see that column in the System Comparison Chart (p. 139) and the individual system descriptions in Part Two.

B. SELECTION

For all the systems the recording task is immense. For most, modifying selection criteria have been established in order to limit somewhat the scope within the coverage of the subjects. Time limits may be established. Some utilize sampling.

Argentina, India, Italy, Morocco, New York City, and Zambia have no time limit. Canada records only pre-1914 buildings. For architecture, France records post-400/pre-1865, plus selected recent buildings. Japan has no established time limit but in practice buildings less than fifty years old are not considered for designation. Mexico has a time limit of 1522–1900 for buildings. Poland generally records pre-1939 buildings (and gardens), rarely those as recent as 1950 and sets 1914 as the cut-off date for wooden construction.

Italy is truly comprehensive with no time limit or selection criteria. Likewise Argentina is gener-

al in approach, selecting entries which are considered to be part of the cultural heritage. Mexican selection is based on local understanding of historical value. France is comprehensive for all architecture entries cited in the *Cadastre Napoléonien* (1805–65) and selective for more recent buildings based on regional sampling. Canada also employs selective sampling. India is selective in only recording centrally protected monuments and sites (see Legal Criteria below) yet comprehensive in that all such entries are recorded.

Similarly, the selective Japanese Ledgers list only designated cultural properties but are comprehensive in that all designated properties are listed. Morocco is comprehensive to record all things but selects only sites and monuments which are 'of the most remarkable examples in the better states of conservation'. New York City is comprehensive for buildings but selective for important urban features. Poland is comprehensive for parks, gardens, avenues and cemeteries, historic cities and towns, and selective, based on expert opinion, for immovable historic monuments. Zambia is comprehensive for archaeological sites and selective for other sites based on citation in source records.

All the methods record existing properties. Canada, New York City, Zambia and France also include entries which were found to be either demolished or destroyed after recording. France cites disappeared constructions as well as unlocatable buildings. Poland includes buildings destroyed or demolished in post-war times which are known from research documentation.

C. LEGAL

Some inventories are designed only to collect information while others provide positive protection. All have a protective aim in varying degrees, sometimes strongly and explicitly expressed, in other cases indirectly and with less force. The legal effects of inclusion vary enormously from one system to another.

Only two systems, the Indian Record and the Japanese Ledger are limited to legally protected entries. For Mexico all entries are protected by being in the Catalogación, while for Morocco classification within the Inventaire National implies legal protection.

More common are the surveys where legal criteria are not emphasized, permitting inclusion of protected and non-protected entries. This is the case for Canada and New York City, although the survey is a tool that may lead to eventual designation of entries either by the Historic Sites and Monuments Board of Canada or by the Landmarks Preservation Commission of New York City.

Argentina includes both protected and non-protected monuments and sites in the SIRAMS.

Monuments and sites are legally protected by municipalities. Currently under study is the possibility that the municipalities could utilize the SIRAMS as a basic preservation tool.

Protected and non-protected buildings and structures are recorded in the French Inventaire Général. It points out buildings or structures that merit protection but has no legal power to protect. This is the duty of the Service des Monuments Historiques.

The Italian Catalogo dei Beni Culturali includes all cultural artefacts, both protected and non-protected. For architecture and urban sectors, legal protection decrees (*vincoli*) are cited by type, number and date. For Poland, inventory documentation provides the basis for planned protection. The Zambia National Site Index includes non-protected, protected, and declared sites.

Worksheet instructions (Criteria)
Clarify all criteria.
A.   *Coverage*. What is the scope of the survey? What subjects will be included. Is the survey comprehensive or selective?
B.   *Selection*. Is every existing example to be included? Is there a cut-off date or time-frame? Is inclusion based on sampling? Will demolished or destroyed examples be included?
C.   *Legal*. Is the survey to record what has been legally protected? Is legal protection implied because of inclusion in the survey? Is the survey a tool to choose what later may be designated for protection?

3. Users and products

Although listed third, this topic could well be first because there would be no inventory or survey if some need for it were not perceived. As such, 'users and products' illustrates excellently the relationship between system components.

In the planning of an inventory system the potential users and their needs should be identified at the beginning, simultaneously with 'purpose and criteria'. Information may be required for staff use, other agencies, researchers or the general public. Different users may need varying levels of data from the components of the survey—basic facts, visual documentation, indepth description, bibliography, etc. 'Products' which will be created to meet these perceived needs should be defined to take account of both Existing Resources (Section 4) and the Method (Section 5).

Because the users and products of the eleven systems present such a diverse and important range of options to be taken into consideration during survey planning, the system-by-system comparison is given below rather than in the brief System Comparison Chart and is followed by Worksheet Instructions for this component.

The following section describes some users and products of the eleven systems. For each official users are noted, including governmental agencies. Special archives or centres to facilitate access to the information are identified. A distinction is made between those systems that stress the importance of the collected forms and their attachments *per se* and those where the information recorded on the forms is of primary importance.

Supportive visual documentation is identified. Published manuals describing the methods themselves are mentioned as are computer indices. For those systems that publish directly, their various publications are elaborated, such as indices, catalogues, monographs, dictionaries and bibliographies.

OFFICIAL USERS

Most of the systems are operated by governmental agencies and, of course, are primarily used by their own staffs. In addition, information is often provided to other governmental agencies as well as to scholars and the general public.

Argentina. SIRAMS is used by staff researchers at the University of Buenos Aires and other preservationists.

Canada. The CIHB provides data for the Historic Sites and Monuments Board as well as to municipal, provincial and national agencies.

France. The Inventaire Général supplies information to government agencies responsible for protection, conservation, restoration and the environment.

India. The Record provides data for the Archaeological Survey staff as well as other regional and central government officials.

Italy. The Catalogo dei Beni Culturali provides data to national, regional and local agencies including police and customs in order to prevent, investigate, and recover illegal exports of cultural artefacts.

Japan. The Ledger of Designated Cultural Property is mainly utilized by national and local government officials.

Mexico. Primarily the staff of the Dirección de Monumentos Historicos make use of the Catalogación Sistema Culhuacán.

Morocco. The Inventaire National is used by the staff of the Ministère d'Etat Chargé des Affaires Culturelles.

New York City. The UCRS furnishes information to the Landmarks Preservation Commission as well as to municipal, state and federal agencies.

Poland. Information is furnished from the five

separate inventories to central and regional agencies.

Zambia. The National Sites Index is used by the staffs of the National Monuments Commission and the Livingstone Museum.

ARCHIVES

All the systems have become repositories for their recorded information; some have, in addition, set up centres to facilitate access to the information.

Canada stores copies of all inventory reports in the national and provincial archives. All recorded data are available to the public at cost, or without charge if they undertake to verify accuracy. Separate office files which contain information on architects, builders and engineers may also be consulted.

France plans documentation centres in Paris and the regions. Open to the general public, each will have a complete set of all microfiche documentation and will provide on-line interrogation with the main computer by means of a CRT terminal and telephone hook-up.

Italy and *Poland*, in particular, have established central documentation centres. The Istituto Centrale per il Catalogo e la Documentazione (ICCD) in Rome and the Historical Monuments Documentation Centre in Warsaw were created to provide standardized methodology and co-ordination and to serve as central collection centres for their particular systems.

Zambia keeps its Site Record Cards in the offices of the National Monuments Commission. These cards contain both computerized and additional information and may be consulted by scholars and students on request.

COLLECTED FORMS

Either the forms and their attachments or the information from the forms, or both, are considered to be primary products of the systems. For many systems the collected recording forms and their attachments of photographic or graphic documentation are perceived as a major resource or product.

Argentina. SIRAMS will attach photos and plans to the forms.

France. Dossiers provide in-depth records of entries in the Inventaire Général. Photographs, plans and photogrammetry as well as texts of bibliography and description are included.

India. The Record describes all centrally protected monuments and sites. Photographs and drawings are attached.

Italy. All 27 categories in the Catalogo have a separate form; a complete visual record of photographs and measured drawings is enclosed within each form.

Japan. The various ledgers provide the sole

official description of all cultural property designated by the nation. Photographs and plans are attached.

Morocco. The Inventaire National includes sites and monuments forms with photographs and plans attached.

Poland. Each of the five separate inventories has its own form; for architecture, photographs and plans are attached.

COLLECTED INFORMATION

For some systems, which are usually computerized, the forms themselves are not as important as the information they contain; the forms are a means and not an end.

Argentina. When computerized it will be the information taken from the forms that will help give the SIRAMS meaning.

France. It is the information gleaned from the *bordereau architecture* that enriches the Inventaire.

Italy. Although not yet computerized, the Catalogo is not considered to be the sum of its forms; it is the total findings that give the individual forms meaning.

Mexico. It is the data taken from the monuments and religious architecture questionnaires that are important.

New York City and *Canada*. Both consider the information on the forms as the substance of the survey, not the actual forms.

Zambia. The computerized data taken from the Site Record Cards become the Index.

VISUAL DOCUMENTATION

One system ignores visual records while the others either accept what they get, use what they have or photograph and draft what they need especially for the project.

Argentina attaches photos and plans to the forms. If none exist they are made. All visual documentation will be eventually stored on microfiches.

France and *Italy* utilize professional graphic documentation, including measured drawings and photogrammetry, in addition to photography. Italy encloses this documentation within the Catalogo form. France keeps originals in dossiers and keyed to the computer data; duplicates are microfiched for easy reproduction and will be available for general use and consultation in the planned documentation centres.

India attaches photos and sketches to the Record and cross-references any additional photos and drawings held in the Circle Office that completed the form.

Japan attaches photographs and maps to the official Ledgers and to the reverse of the Record of Investigation card as well.

Mexico has collected photographs and plans from volunteer recorders if they chose to send them.

Morocco attaches plans, photographs and drawings to the site/monument forms. A separate photo index (*photothèque*) allows retrospective research on all entries in the Inventaire National.

New York City and *Canada* photograph every entry on black-and-white 35 mm film and attach contact prints to photo cards for office reference. In addition the film-roll number and frames are computerized by New York so that automatic indices of photographs are possible.

Poland photographs on black-and-white film for the Inventory Sheet and includes plans drawn to a set scale and maps. The Archaeological Map of Poland uses graphic symbols to represent information visually.

Zambia. Since it was based on known sources without further field-work, the Site Index does not include photographs.

COMPUTER INDICES

All systems which are currently computerized can search, sort and list the data.

France uses three programs specially developed for the Inventaire Général: EDI CART, to provide a distribution map of points in each commune of a canton; EDI FICH, to print data on cards; and EDI CANT, to list each canton sorted by place name and subject.

Mexico provides listings by type of building or monument, date and location.

New York City and *Canada* have flexible formats for data where any question(s), answer(s), or combination(s), can be searched, sorted and listed in any sequence.

MANUALS

All the systems use their own special form(s); several have manuals or lexicons that describe their methodology and define the questions. Some of these also provide a standard vocabulary of answer terms which helps to ensure a homogeneous product. Only one manual is illustrated.

Argentina anticipates completing a manual for SIRAMS by July 1982.

Canada has published a detailed, illustrated *Exterior Recording Training Manual* that defines the recording method and all standard coded answers. Instructions for mapping and photography are also provided. Their Selection Form also includes schematic illustrations which graphically illustrate most answer choices. This didactic form teaches an architectural nomenclature particularly useful for training volunteers.

France describes the recording method using the *bordereau architecture* in a detailed manual,

Lexique de la Zone 1 pour architecture. This includes a standard vocabulary of terms.

Italy has published a set of all the forms used in the *Repertorio delle schede di catalogo dei beni culturali*. Two manuals provide directives. One covers artistic and historic works; the other immovable objects. *Norme per la redazione delle schede di catalogo dei beni culturali, beni artistici e storici* and . . . *beni immobile*.

Mexico describes the methodology of the Catalogación Sistema Culhuacán as part of a published print-out index. *Sistematización de Datos*, which clarifies the questions, is included within the indices *Monumentos y lugares de belleza natural* and *Arquitectura religiosa* . . .

Morocco has no lexicon but the *Nomenclature typologique* is a standard vocabulary of coded uses; many are Arabic terms.

New York City explains the UCRS methodology in *Notes* which details instructions for completing the form; *Codes* lists all questions and precoded answers in a standard vocabulary.

Poland has described the various methodologies, except for archaeology, in *A System for Inventorying Historical Monuments in Poland*. All questions are defined.

Zambia provides 'Notes on Entries' which describes the methodology in *A Classified Index of Archaeological and Other Sites in Zambia*, which is a print-out index.

PUBLICATIONS

Information and illustrative documentation from each system may be provided to other governmental agencies or to scholars for their own research and publication. However, several of the systems publish directly. These publications include computerized indices, catalogues, monographs, dictionaries and bibliographies.

Published information may be taken directly from recorded data (computerized indices) or it may be an analysis of recorded material (catalogues and monographs). Bibliographies are published from reference citations. Specialized dictionaries are based upon the lexicons of terms originally developed to clarify methodology. Often illustrations for the publications come direct from collected visual documentation. These publications help increase public sensitivity to the heritage and, in turn, public awareness of the system itself. They not only serve to heighten a sense of the past which cultural properties represent but also to establish or affirm a sense of identification with the physical evidence of that past.

UNILLUSTRATED COMPUTERIZED INDICES

France 'To publicize' is one objective of the Inventaire Général. One means to this end is the

Indicateur du patrimoine published directly from computerized data in topographic order with multiple indices.

Mexico. Both the *Monumentos y lugares de belleza natural* and *Arquitectura religiosa . . .* are print-out listings from the Catalogación Sistema Culhuacán. Brief location information and general characteristics are provided. These listings are considered to be only the basis for later analytic catalogues.

Zambia. A *Classified Index of Archaeological and Other Sites* is a computerized print-out listing 1,543 sites. Originally published in 1976; a revised version appeared in 1978. Sites are listed by province, name, category and type, etc. Multiple indices are included.

CATALOGUES AND MONOGRAPHS

Based on analyses and interpretations of recorded data, catalogues and monographs are generally illustrated.

Canada has prepared detailed studies on building types, materials and technology, and the origin of building styles.

France describes the findings of the Inventaire Général by canton in the serial publication *Inventaire topographique.* Every work studied is included. These are abundantly illustrated.

Italy. Topographic catalogues and indices are planned for the Catalogo dei Beni Culturali.

Morocco. The Inventaire National has published a study of rock art in southern Morocco based on an analysis of recorded data: *Catalogue des sites rupestres du Sud Marocain.*

Poland has published monographs on special subjects such as timber churches, also conservation and construction techniques.

BIBLIOGRAPHIES

Bibliographic references collected during recording have been published as reference sources.

France. The *Répertoires des inventaires* provide analytic bibliography by region, department and category of works. This series is based upon the bibliography collected within the dossiers of the Inventaire Général.

Morocco. The *Fichier-Index bibliographique du patrimoine* is a computerized bibliography covering all Moroccan cultural heritage. (A separate *Microthèque* contains microfiche documents.)

DICTIONARIES

Definitions of terms that were established to clarify the methodology have been published as specialized dictionaries.

France has published a two-volume illustrated *Vocabulaire de l'architecture*, a scientific analysis and definition of terms. Additional *Vocabulaires* for sculpture, tapestries, objects, furniture and paintings will soon appear.

Italy has begun a general series of historic lexicons under the general title of 'Dizionari terminologici'. The first volume covers archaeological materials from the last Bronze Age to the first Iron Age: *Materiali dell'età del bronze e della prima età del ferro.*

Poland has also published dictionaries of special terms.

INTANGIBLE PRODUCTS

In addition to the tangible products of these systems there are intangibles. Those systems that use volunteers and, particularly non-professional volunteers, as in Mexico, Canada and New York City, may have gained community or local support and interest for their work as well as helped to make the volunteers more conscious of their own environment.

Worksheet instructions (Users and products)

Identify the potential users. What are their needs and what survey products will satisfy these needs? Define the separate components of these needs or products (basic data, photographs, bibliography, etc.). Are some needs or components more important than others? Can these be considered basic? Where is the collected information to be used? Who will have access to it? Will the information be indexed? Will the user directly interrogate the data? Is visual documentation necessary? Of what quality? Is a staff manual needed? Will there be publications directly from the survey such as indices, catalogues, monographs, dictionaries or bibliographies?

4. Existing resources

By resources we mean manpower (central and field staff, and volunteers), assistance from other organizations, and tapping outside sources for information and expertise. For computer expertise see Method (Section 5) below.

A. STAFF

The selection and skills of office and data-collection personnel are crucial to conducting an accurate and professional survey. While there is always a central office staff, it may not perform the majority of the recording work. Some systems use field or regional personnel to send completed information to headquarters. The following systems rely heavily on field recorders for data collection:

Canada. Seasonal field recorders send information to the Ottawa headquarters of the CIHB for final processing.

France. The Inventaire Général divides work between Paris and regional offices. Archaeological information is collected by the Service des Fouilles Archéologiques.

India. Work is done by regional Circle Offices' personnel and sent to the central office of the Archaeological Survey in New Delhi.

Italy. Information is gathered regionally by various departments (*soprintendenze*) of the Ministerio per il Beni Culturali e Ambientali or the Ministerio della Pubblica Istruzione. The Instituto Centrale per il Catalogo e la Documentazione provides method and co-ordination as well as serving as the central archive.

Japan. The central office collects the information for the Ledger of Designated Cultural Property. For immovable properties work is actually done by the staff of the Architecture and Monuments Divisions of the Agency for Cultural Affairs.

Poland. The recording method is centrally organized, planned and supervised by the Historic Monuments Documentation Centre but is carried out in the field under the direction of regional Voivodship offices.

In *Argentina, New York City, Morocco* and *Zambia* the central office staff does most of the recording work.

In addition to field-work some systems rely on published sources for data collection. The Zambian National Site Index is based on the pre-existence of records in available known sources without further field-work. For sites and monuments the Inventaire National of *Morocco* is based on preliminary analytic studies, then site visits using as a reference the prepared studies. For France the *Cadastre Napoléonien* (1805–65) is used as the comprehensive reference tool for architecture. Site visits may occur but are not necessary for recording.

B. VOLUNTEERS

Many of the systems utilize volunteers both as a working method and for economy. Volunteer labour is considered to be free. However, what is gained must be weighed against accuracy and the need for staff to check or recode the information as well as the cost of training.

Argentina. The SIRAMS utilizes volunteer university students from the University of Buenos Aires.

Canada. The CIHB has been assisted by volunteers. Its distinctive grid format was designed to teach a nomenclature of architecture for non-professional use. An architectural recording course is provided if necessary.

France. Some volunteers assist in the regions. All volunteer assistance, however, is reviewed by staff.

Italy. The Catalogo uses about 1,000 volunteers with particular skills who work on individual assignments.

Mexico. The Catalogación made greatest and most systematic use of volunteer assistance, receiving help from more than 7,500 parish priests and municipal delegates who recorded the data and sent them to the central office where staff coded them for computerization. This volunteer recording system did not work, however, in large urban centres.

New York City. The Urban Cultural Resources Survey utilizes volunteer assistance. There is a three-session training programme for volunteers who may be high-school and college students or local residents.

C. OUTSIDE ASSISTANCE AND RESOURCES

Collaboration may be established with other institutions to provide development assistance or provide information and codes. Argentina has utilized the resources of the Instituto de Arte Americano 'Mario J. Buschiazzo' in the development of the SIRAMS. The French Inventaire notes those buildings which have been protected (or should be) by the Service des Monuments Historiques another *sous-direction* of the same ministry. The Mexican Catalogación Sistema Culhuacán has received the official collaboration of several institutes for providing expertise.

Codes used by other institutions are incorporated into the systems of: Argentina (the ENCOTEL mail and telegraph code); France and Morocco (Lambert cartographic zones); Italy (Automobile Club abbreviations for the province); Mexico (municipality codes used by the Dirección General de Estadistica); and New York City (Master Street List used by every city department).

Worksheet instructions (Existing resources)
A.   *Staff.* Identify the necessary and available human resources. Will there be a central office plus regional staff? Need staff be especially recruited or trained? Will site visits be necessary? If so provide staff identification.
B.   *Volunteers.* Could volunteer assistance be used to collect data? What is the means to recruit volunteers? Need volunteers be trained?
C.   *Outside Assistance.* Identify other existing resources such as other institutes, agencies, services. Can any of these be used? Should any of these be used? Must any of these be

used for 'political' reasons? What systems exist to which the survey should be made compatible?

5. Method

If surveys bring order to a dispersed and endangered world of cultural properties, then survey method has the parallel task of organizing the chaos of facts which exist in that world. Standardization and computerization help organize this chaos. Since the basic decision for Method is whether or not the system should be manual or computerized, a short discussion within this section first sets out the pros and cons of computerization in layman's terms. This is followed by some considerations, for both manual and computerized systems, regarding the need for standardization.

COMPUTERIZATION

All but two of the inventory methodologies described either use or plan to use computers. However, the type and amount of information each system collects and inputs, as well as the manner in which they output data, differ. Each has specific limitations and advantages.

General background (key terms in italics)

For computerization the basic process is to collect information in a standard manner, punch it on to magnetic tape or disc and put it into computer memory using an operating language. To manipulate the input within the computer (*hardware*) one uses certain *programs (software)* which provide output for the user.

Information is collected on a standard form in a series of questions; each question is called a *field*. Forms are standard so that the same type of information is always found in the same field. Each field is assigned a particular location on the computer tape or disc composed of a specific series of *spaces* called *bytes*.

Spaces (or bytes)

The number of spaces accords with the size of the possible answer. All fields for each entry make up the total *record* or *entry*. The entry length may be fixed at a predetermined number of spaces or be left open. For example, Zambia and New York City have fixed entry lengths of 53 spaces and 560 spaces respectively, while France has a fixed length of 800 spaces which can be further expanded or opened.

Several entries input at the same time are called a *batch*. All the entries for any one method make up the total *data base* which may comprise several separate files or sub-sets.

Until recently computer entry was by eighty-space cards; each card comprised one *line* of data. Some systems still use eighty-space data lines;

others may divide data into lines of varying length. New York City utilizes seven lines of eighty spaces; France has twenty lines of forty spaces. Each line may code information for several fields.

Lines

The simplest computer method (used by Mexico and Zambia) is limited to one line of data per entry. Each line represents a new entry and is divided into coded fields for various questions. Such a method is inexpensive to input, store and process. Updating and changing data is easy since these are relatively 'small' data bases utilizing one line per entry (1,500 entries for Zambia; 13,000 for Mexico).

More complex methods (Canada, France, Morocco and New York City) use several lines per entry. Each of these lines needs to be identified in order to determine what kind of information (what fields) are stored on that line. Both Morocco and New York City preprint the line number on the entry form. Morocco calls the line number the c.c. number; New York the record number. France uses the question number to identify the line.

All the lines of data that comprise an entry for one object must be identified as belonging together by means of a *unique identifier* for each entry. Thus New York City repeats the geocode on each line of the entry; Morocco repeats the type-order number.

Both the line numbers and the unique identifier (entry number) always occur in the same fields on every line.

Codes

Information may be entered within each field as *free text* (ordinary words), as *keywords* (standard coded vocabularies) or as *alpha-numerics* (coded letters and numbers). Each of these types has particular advantages and limitations based on factors of comprehensibility, length and cost.

Computerization cost is based on a combination of collection, data entry or input, storage, processing and output costs. The longer the entry and the greater the quantity of entries the more expensive data is to input, store and process; the terser entry has the advantage of being the cheapest.

Alpha-numerics

Tersest of all are alpha-numeric codes. The simplest of these, for example, is a '1' or '0' response if data is (1) or is not (0) present. Zambia uses this to code the existence of Carbon-14 dates and Mexico to code the existence of a church porch. In addition, combined digits can represent up to 99 possibilities in two spaces, 999 in three spaces, etc. Such codes either need to be predetermined or assigned sequentially. Canada uses both a standard predetermined code for each province (two digits) and a sequential numeric of four digits to represent each town.

Coded alpha-numerics are not easily comprehensible to the user unless he is extremely familiar with the method. Usually the coded answers will be decoded either manually by the user or automatically by a program.

Keywords

A less terse level of coding uses standard vocabularies or keywords. The choice of answer is limited only to those keywords. They may be arranged hierarchically in a thesaurus. The French list of *dénominations* is hierarchical; the Moroccan *nomenclature typologique* is not.

Keywords are often more acceptable to the recorder than alpha-numerics and are always more easily understood by the user. However, the development of appropriate thesauri of terms can be time consuming.

Keyword storage within computer memory generally requires more space than alpha-numerics with a consequent higher cost for entry, storage and processing. Thus for economy keywords may be stored as numeric codes and programmed to print out as words. Canada and New York City do this for most questions and Mexico and Zambia for some. When the information is entered and stored numerically, however, it cannot be interrogated easily by a user who is unfamiliar with the codes. France enters and stores keywords as words and, thus, has a system which can be more readily interrogated.

Free text

The most expensive type of entry is free text. This uses far more space than either alpha-numerics or keywords. It is useful, however, for such questions as place names, building names, architects, etc., where the terms will be discovered as the system develops. France, Mexico, Morocco, and Zambia all enter the actual name of the monument or site in free text. Such individual terms in free text can be searched within set fields.

Complex statements or passages can also be entered as free text. France gives historical commentary in this manner; Argentina plans to include text. Since long text passages contain non-predetermined (i.e. free) words in non-set fields they require far more complex and expensive computer programs for processing.

Commands and output

Coded data is keypunched from forms on to magnetic tape or disc for input by means of the computer system's *operating language*. Once the data are input they are manipulated by means of certain commands and specialized programs.

Some commands are basic to all operating languages such as those which automatically alphabetize and numerically order data within set fields. Other kinds of manipulation for searching and selecting need to be especially programmed either using the operating language or a program (software) package designed for that task.

In Canada and New York City special programs were written to search for all numeric entries with any specified characteristics. A software package, MARK IV, is normally used to generate reports or output in English or French from the numerically stored data. Since much of these data are stored *off-line* (i.e. not immediately accessible), the report may take several hours to process. Other special programs may produce output for particular purposes such as the French EDI CART (distribution map of points in each commune), EDI FICH (print data on cards), and EDI CANT (canton sorted by place name and subject). In whatever form the data may be needed a program can generally either be found or be written to output them for all systems.

In some systems the request for data is made to a separate data-processing unit which, in turn, provides *hard copy print out* (listings on paper). In other methods either a technician or the user himself may program the request using an office *CRT terminal* (video-screen and keyboard) hooked up via a telephone line to the main data base. The resulting output may be either displayed on the screen of the terminal or printed as hard copy.

In New York City, staff and researchers must ask the system specialist to program each request since the data base cannot be easily interrogated by non-computer specialists. In France, however, staff may directly interrogate the data base in an easily understood conversational mode. The public also will be able to interrogate the data in Paris and the regions at planned documentation centres by means of additional terminals linked to the main data base.

Pros and cons

It is inconceivable that computerization should not be considered for any inventory begun today. Even 'small' systems with as few as 1,000 entries modified by 10 questions comprise 10,000 items of data, and this is too large for any manual method to attempt to manipulate properly.

Few terminologies are too specialized to be computerized. Unique words can always be entered as free text although even the most esoteric terms, if considered objectively, can be adopted to the confines of a hierarchy to ease computer processing.

Professional help is available. None of the systems discussed has been developed in isolation. Data processing is always handled by a separate unit or department which provides the actual computers and professional engineering and programming skills.

Nevertheless, there are limitations to computerization. Generally information must be collected in a standard manner, using set codes of established terms. For manual methodologies that have been in existence for years this rigid standardization may be difficult to apply. Codes need to be defined and established. Hierarchical thesauri take time to produce. Time is also necessary to write or develop specialized programs and to learn to use existing software packages.

Once collected some information may need to be periodically changed or updated. For large files with entries of many lines this can be a difficult and tedious process, since the data may be stored on several tapes or discs. Errors or changes need to be located, corrected and copied as 'cleaned' on to another tape or disc.

How data are stored and made available also causes limitations. In cheaper *time-sharing* systems (where several clients share the same computer) each has his own tapes or discs. These need to be mounted and made ready in order to interrogate the entire data base. This takes time. In an expensive *dedicated* system all data belong to the one user and is generally on-line; there is no time delay.

Not all data are easy to understand. Information that has been coded for economical storage needs to be decoded for general use either manually by the user or automatically by a program. In New York City and Canada where information is stored as numerics, on-line data are always in code. User-readable print-out either in English or French must be produced in an off-line batch program which may take hours.

The greatest limitation is perhaps the ordinary human difficulty in using systems. Not all systems are user oriented; nor are they *interactive* or designed to be directly interrogated in a conversational mode. In Zambia and Mexico all requests are made through the data-processing unit. In Canada and New York City requests are made through the system specialist who programs the request. In France the data base is stored as keywords which staff can, and the public will, interrogate in an easily understood conversational mode.

In spite of these limitations computerization remains an extraordinary means for information retrieval and use. Obvious positive aspects include the speed with which data can be searched, sorted and retrieved; the low cost relative to the effort and expense of professional data collection; the multiple levels of use from the same data according to the levels of user request; the almost limitless comparisons and contrasts which are possible within the data itself; and the pure intellectual delight of discovering new relations between the facts and concepts of the recorded cultural heritage.

STANDARDIZATION

Forms and formats

All systems, both computerized and manual, are dependent on organization of their collected facts. The use of forms is the beginning of the organization process because forms systematize information in a standard manner that repeats itself from one entry to the next. Examples of many forms from the eleven systems have been reproduced within this Manual. The actual questions on these forms are, of course, discussed in Part Three (Question comparison) and the schematic Question Typology Chart.

A preliminary form can be designed once coverage criteria are established and a rough idea is known about how the information will be used. These factors (Nos. 2 and 3 on the Planning Worksheet) determine the information levels required or the breadth and depth of the inquiry. In the Question Typology Chart (page 145) three levels are identified: Primary, Secondary and Optional.

Primary questions are virtually mandatory for all surveys, whatever their objectives or resources. The Secondary questions give a survey its emphasis. For example, Canada's twenty-six questions about physical building description (Analytic Chart 4F) alerts us to the fact that the basic objective of this survey is to record the architectural heritage. Japan's nine questions about designation of Preservation Districts (Analytic Chart 2B) denotes its strong legal emphasis. See the Synthesis Grid for a graphic illustrations of this (page 149). Optional questions are felt necessary by some systems, but often the effort to collect this information accurately is not cost-effective.

The ideal form is a sheet of questions which, filled in, is immediately readable and usable for reference yet automatically indexed or coded for computerization without redrafting. Zambia's Site Record Card is one example of such a form.

Short and long formats

Recognizing the impossibility of studying all cultural property at the same depth many systems, for convenience, divide their information into necessary and additional, basic and descriptive, or short and long formats.

France has a minimal computerized record (PIN) for all entries plus in-depth supporting dossiers of visual and textual documentation.

India uses a brief list and an in-depth record to describe the same centrally protected monuments and sites.

Italy records detailed information but plans to computerize only basic questions.

Japan keeps detailed official ledgers for designated cultural properties plus the brief Record of

Investigation on cards for archaeological and historic sites with non-excavated remains.

Mexico records briefly all monuments and places, including religious buildings, and has a separate more comprehensive form for only religious architecture.

Morocco will computerize basic information on the Liste Générale and manually records comprehensive descriptions for each site and monument.

Poland uses a brief address form for basic data on each object exhibiting some historical features or values and elaborates this with separate in-depth inventory sheets.

Zambia has basic computerized questions for each entry with additional non-computerized material inscribed on the reverse.

Vocabulary and procedure

Essential to all systems are the considerations of standardization of vocabulary and procedure. Vocabulary standards can be as simple as the list of words encountered in describing a given type of property or as complex as a hierarchically arranged thesaurus of defined terms. The vocabulary for both can be drawn from the forms during data collection, but preparing thesauri can be a long process better suited to fully computerized systems where the terminology will assist in later automatic retrieval of the data.

Another useful, if not essential, aid for production of a homogeneous survey, when more than one person is collecting the data, is a manual or handbook, which describes each question on the form(s) and how to answer it. In addition these may provide a range of possible answers. System manuals or handbooks are further discussed above in 'Users and Products' (Section 3).

One further consideration for method is updating. The work in many systems can or never should be considered finished. New entries are added as well as corrections and changes made within the recorded information. Updating itself needs to be planned and budgeted as well as primary recording. The method must accommodate these changes.

Worksheet instructions (Method)
A. *Computerization.* To determine if and how the survey may be computerized, talk with a professional programmer. Find out what operating languages and programs (software) are available as well as their advantages, disadvantages, and requirements. Consider the various kinds of entry—alpha-numeric codes, keywords, and free text—against the factors of economy and comprehensibility. Calculate the length required

for each entry and the total number of entries considered for each system. Remember that although you may design the data-collection form and code it, you will need professional programming assistance.
B. *Standardization.* Determine how many forms will be used. Will there be a standardized vocabulary for answers? Is a manual necessary to clarify the procedure and define terms? Does updating need to be built into the method?

6. Costs and time

Costs for the survey as well as the time necessary to complete the effort can vary enormously, depending upon planning decisions taken about the purpose, criteria, products, staff and method. The section on Statistics in the System Comparison Chart and in the individual system descriptions of Part Two give a general idea of these factors for each of the eleven systems discussed within the Manual.

Nevertheless, every system plan needs to estimate the time necessary to acquire the information levels desired, including start-up time for development, testing and modification. Some systems may need to identify (and acquire) the funds necessary to complete the work.

In light of the pragmatic realities of costs and time the desired methodology may need to be re-evaluated and modified. For example, limited funds may require that data be collected from prior publications or by volunteers instead of paid staff.

Whatever the actual purpose, criteria, products, resources, method and costs an ideal system methodology should be designed so that work can be started before all factors are known (they can never be all known entirely anyway) and evolve during the recording process. One should be able to test the system, then modify and improve it until the variable factors are under control. No inventory, however didactic or scholarly, can re-create the actual cultural property. The purpose is to provide the users with an 'image' of that property—information—that will aid in studying, understanding and ultimately, perhaps, protecting it.

Worksheet instructions (Costs and time).
Estimate the time necessary to acquire the primary, secondary and optional information levels desired. Calculate the cost. Compare with the funds available. Re-evaluate the first five points of the Planning Worksheet in light of these realities and modify the methodology if necessary.

Part Two

System description

Introduction

In order to help the reader examine the eleven systems in the Manual, the description of each follows a standardized format. A System Comparison Chart(page 139) summarizes some of this information. A full Discussion of the system's major components is followed by a Summary/ Evaluation. The Question Analysis and its Appendix deals with the actual questions asked.[1] These four sections are described below.

In the Discussion section:

Objectives and statistics state the purpose and aims, date established, anticipated date of completion, number of entries as of 31 December 1980, and costs.

Staff gives the number and professions of personnel and any volunteer assistance.

Criteria describes the kinds of subjects included, any cut-off date or time-frame, the level of legal protection, whether the inventory is comprehensive or selective and how selection is made.

Method covers the format and form(s), the working language, any lexicon or manual and special instructions.

Computerization specifies programming languages, software, record format, type of entry and storage.

Users and products notes the agencies or groups which utilize the data, the level of information available, and the resulting lists, photographs, drawings and publications.

The Summary/Evaluation section identifies briefly the strengths and weaknesses of the system.

The Question Analysis section considers all questions from the forms included in the Manual. In order to compare and contrast each question type in a standard manner questions have been placed in a thematic and logical framework of seven main categories.

These seven categories have the following functions:

1. *Identification/location* names the entry, classifies the type or use, geographically locates it, cites cartographic co-ordinates or property registration, and notes ownership.

2. *Significance/designation* evaluates the importance or merit and specifies present level of official designation and other legalities, citing decree, date, etc., as well as proposing any future level.

3. *Date/history* provides the date of the entry, discusses building history, construction campaigns, associated events, legends and traditions. Authorship is identified.

4. *Description* details the general area and setting as well as the particular site and structure. Dimensions, general accounts, style, material, technique, elements, immovable and movable features are noted.

5. *Conservation/restoration/preservation* describes the present condition, past maintenance work and future perspective and practices.

6. *Documentation/reference* cites published bibliography, files and reports, maps, plans and drawings, as well as photographs including microfiche. Any attachments or enclosures are noted. Archival information, contingencies and cross-references to other forms within the system are given.

7. *Systematization* includes the recording record which notes the date and source or compiler of the form as well as any site inspection and systematics which organize the recorded information.

1. Facsimiles of original documents can be found at the end of the Manual.

The Appendix section lists the questions in their original sequence on the forms analysed. Where necessary questions have been translated into English. Copies of many of the original forms are also reproduced as well as selected other materials.

Argentina (AR)

Sistema Automatizado de Inventario y Registro de Monumentos y Sitios (SIRAMS)

Based on information supplied by
Carlos Pernaut, Director.

Discussion

OBJECTIVES AND STATISTICS

The Sistema Automatizado de Inventario y Registro de Monumentos y Sitios is sponsored by the University of Buenos Aires. There are four objectives: (a) to inventory and catalogue in a technical and systematic manner the urban and rural monumental heritage of Argentina; (b) to create and keep archives up to date while allowing registration of cultural objects; (c) to produce simultaneous translations of texts and recorded information; and (d) to interrogate thematically the inventory data. The first two objectives are under way on an experimental level; the last two are under study.

The initial objective was that there would be 180 monuments and 10 sites or ensembles recorded within the Sistema. Various sources have contributed funds and resources for the experimental stage and exact costs cannot be calculated.

It is planned that the system will have the capability to interrogate data by combining questions, as well as the simultaneous translation of texts and recorded information from Spanish into English and French. It is predicted that by December 1983 SIRAMS will have the capability to interrogate the data base thematically.

STAFF

Professional staff for the Sistema total fifteen and include: two architects, one computer engineer, six researchers and six technicians specialized in linguistics, data entry and programming. In addition, fifteen to twenty university students from the Faculty of Architecture and Urbanism of the University of Buenos Aires are acting as volunteers.

Volunteer training sessions have been organized regularly since 1976 and co-ordinated under the auspices of the Unesco Youth Participation Programme in Conservation of Landscape and Cultural Heritage. Staff researchers and historians from the Instituto de Arte Americano 'Mario J. Buschiazzo' also collaborate on the project.

CRITERIA

The system is selective; only those monuments and sites (including ensembles) considered to be part of the cultural heritage are recorded. In addition, underwater and industrial archaeology are also covered on separate forms. There is no cut-off date for entries.

Both protected and non-protected entries are cited. Monuments and sites are under the legal protection of municipalities who pass their own ordinances, decrees and codes. Federal laws are under study at present in an effort to see how the municipalities can utilize SIRAMS as a basic preservation tool.

METHOD

The system began with forms designed for manual use. The Council of Europe model was originally adopted. Following trials throughout the country, the form was redesigned to meet Argentine needs and to be compatible with the Colombian format.

After a meeting in 1976 of the Presidents of the ICOMOS National Committees of the Southern Cone Region of Latin America, a common recording form was established for the region. Experimental testing has been completed in the San Isidro Conservation Area, Buenos Aires Province.

It is anticipated that once the format is finalized

a manual will be prepared. Separate forms record monuments and sites. The monument form contains twenty-four numbered questions; the site form, sixteen. Entry will be in keywords. Recording is done from a combination of site visits, office files and bibliography.

COMPUTERIZATION

Computerization of the SIRAMS is now under development. Assistance for the experimental stages of the system has been provided by the Computer Centre at the University of Buenos Aires.

The programming language is COBOL. It is anticipated that both the capability to interrogate the system by a combination of questions as well as the translation program using SYSTRAM will be operational soon. This simultaneous translation program of texts and recorded information from Spanish into English and French will facilitate a wider use and greater exchange of the information. It is anticipated also that the system will be compatible with STAIRS, for thematic interrogation of the data base.

USERS AND PRODUCTS

For all three computer programs, print-out listings, as well as visual display of data by means of CRT terminals hooked up to the main data base, will be available for the user. Microfiche will also provide documentation.

Summary/Evaluation

The Argentine Sistema Automatizado de Inventario y Registro de Monumentos y Sitios is a methodology which will be computerized to inventory and catalogue the monumental heritage of the country. Criteria are selective and include only those monuments and sites that are considered to be part of the cultural heritage. There is no time limit on entries.

Separate forms are used to record monuments and sites. Emphasis is placed on the legal protection and conservation state. For monuments, possible future adaptability, as well as financing, are given particular consideration. Bibliography, plans and photographs are included.

Microfiches are planned to be combined with a computer index utilizing several programs. One program will interrogate the data base by a combination of questions, another will provide thematic interrogation and a third will allow simultaneous translation of recorded information and texts.

Question analysis

An analysis of the kinds of information asked on the separate monument and site forms follows. The analysis is by question and not by the question sequence on the forms. For a question-by-question comparison of these Argentine questions contrasted with the other systems see Part Three.

INDENTIFICATION/LOCATION

Both the Monument and Site forms name the entry and cite its location by province, region, ENCOTEL, district, section, ilot or block and particular address. The ENCOTEL is the standard postal and telegraph code for the country. The monument form also asks for present-use plus proposed-use.

SIGNIFICANCE/DESIGNATION

For monuments the level of significance (*grado de valor*) is evaluated. Both the level of present legal protection as well as proposed protection is given. For sites the extent of protection and the type is noted.

DATE/HISTORY

For both forms chronological evolution is stated. For monuments the date on which work commenced and was completed is indicated, as well as the name of the chief of the project (*proyectista*).

DESCRIPTION

No questions provide for a physical description of either entry.

CONSERVATION/RESTORATION/PRESERVATION

Both forms detail the conservation condition. In addition, for monuments, the possible level of adaptability for future use and level of investment are suggested.

DOCUMENTATION/REFERENCE

Both forms cite bibliography as well as reference plans and photographs. Bibliography comprises books, publications and others; the plan specifies the ensemble, floors, details, cross-sections, façade and perspectives; photograph types allow for interior, exterior and aerial. If no plans or photographs exist, they are made. Both plans and photographs are attached to the forms. Documentation will also be stored on microfiches.

Recording record

No questions cover this topic

SYSTEMATIZATION

Systematics
Each individual entry is assigned a unique coded inventory number. Cross-reference is made to separate microfiche numbers.

Appendix

ORIGINAL QUESTION SEQUENCE
AND TRANSLATION (FORM AR1)[1]

Monumento	Monument
1. Número de inventario	Inventory number
2. Provincia	Province
3. Región	Region
4. ENCOTEL	ENCOTEL
5. Circunscripción	District
6. Sección	Section
7. Manzana	Ilot or block
8. Ubicación	Address
9. Denominación	Name
10. Proyectista	Chief of project
11. Fecha de inicio	Date of initiation
12. Fecha de terminación	Date of completion
13. Utilización existente	Present use
14. Utilización propuesta	Proposed use
15. Estado de conservación	Conservation condition
16. Grado de protección existente	Level of present protection
17. Grado de protección propuesta	Level of proposed protection
18. Grado de valor	Level of importance
19. Grado de adaptabilidad	Level of adaptability
20. Grado de inversión	Level of investment
21. Evolución, datos cronológicos	Evolution, chronology
22. Bibliografía	Bibliography
Libros	Books
Revistas	Publications
Otros	Other
23. Planos de conjunto	Plans of ensemble
Plantas	Floors
Detalles	Details
Cortes	Cross-sections
Vistas	Views
Perspectivas	Perspectives
24. Fotografías	Photographs
Interiores	Interior
Exteriores	Exterior
Aéreas	Aerial

ORIGINAL QUESTIONS SEQUENCE
AND TRANSLATION (FORM AR2)

Sitio	*Site*
1. Número de inventario	Inventory number
2. Provincia	Province
3. Región	Region
4. ENCOTEL	ENCOTEL
5. Circunscripción	District
6. Sección	Section
7. Manzana	Ilot or block
8. Denominación	Name
9. Ubicación	Address
10. Protección—extensión	Extent of protection
11. Tipo de protección	Type of protection
12. Estado de conservación	Conservation condition
13. Evolución, datos cronológicos	Evolution, chronology
14. Bibliografía	Bibliography
Libros	Books
Revistas	Publications
Otros	Other
15. Planos de conjunto	Plans of ensemble
Plantas	Floors
Detalles	Details
Cortes	Cross-sections
Vistas	Views
Perspectivas	Perspectives
16. Fotografías	Photographs
Interiores	Interior
Exteriores	Exterior
Aéreas	Aerial

1. No facsimile is included for this document.

Canada (CA)

Canadian Inventory of Historic Building (CIHB)

Based on information supplied by
B. A. Humphreys, Chief

Discussion

OBJECTIVES AND STATISTICS

The Canadian Inventory of Historic Building is a programme of the National Historic Parks and Sites Branch, Parks Canada, Department of Indian and Northern Affairs. It was primarily designed to provide data to enable the Historic Sites and Monuments Board to judge the significance of a building or a group of buildings by comparison with others of similar features and values. That assessment process would culminate in the designation of some outstanding examples as National Historic Sites and Monuments. However, the CIHB has become a data source for all groups interested in the Canadian architectural heritage.

The programme is carried out in several phases. Phase 1 records the exteriors of pre-1914 buildings using 35 mm black-and-white photographs and a standard recording form which codes location and common design features for computer input. In Phase 2 the interiors of a selection of the buildings identified in Phase 1 are detailed. Phase 3 consists of in-depth documentary research of selected buildings.

Systematic exterior recording began in summer 1970. As from 31 December 1980, more than 169,000 building exteriors had been recorded across Canada and this work is continuing. Records of structures discovered to have been demolished after surveying are later updated to note that fact. Neither the date of completion nor the final total of entries can be foreseen. New entries average between 5,000 and 10,000 per year. The annual computer budget is C$45,000; the cost per entry is approximately C$15 when field and headquarters staff time and expenses are included.

STAFF

A full-time professional headquarters staff of twelve directs the efforts of between twenty and a hundred seasonal field recorders and photographers who are hired periodically each year and an additional twenty to fifty volunteers who provide assistance. Seasonal field recording is due to the severe climatic conditions of the country; on-site recording is generally impossible in winter.

CRITERIA

The CIHB is selective. A sample of existing pre-1914 building exteriors are located and recorded. Headquarters staff selects the areas to be surveyed; the field recorders locate and record on site all buildings thought to meet the criteria. Both designated and non-designated buildings are recorded.

METHOD

The forms

Recording is done on the site. The method (bilingual in English and French) is fully described in the *Exterior Recording Training Manual/Guide de description de l'architecture extérieure*. All questions and answer possibilities are defined; many are multiple-choice. Most are illustrated. Instructions for mapping and photography are also provided. Two forms are used. Both ask the same questions, the first to help the recorder visually to select building features, the second simply to mark the coded answers.

The selection form (8½ × 14 inches—216 × 356 mm) consists of a cover sheet and nine pages of schematic drawings on a grid which graphically illustrate most answer choices. Correct choices are visually identified by comparing what is drawn on the form with what exists on the site. Separate selection forms are provided in English and French.

The recording form is a single card folded into a cover sheet and a computer form (8½ × 14 inches—216 × 356 mm). The computer form prints all question numbers and answer spaces. The recorder writes in the correct numeric code for most questions; for some questions multiple-choice answers are preprinted and these are checked off. In order to use the bilingual recording form, the recorder must be familiar with the method, questions and answers.

Photography

Both the selection form and the recording form have a cardboard cover sheet on which location information is given. The bottom of the cover sheet is perforated to make a separate photo card. This is detached at the headquarters and stored in the office files.

Generally at least six photographs are taken. The first must be an identification picture in which the top two-thirds of the cover sheet is legible with its location information completed in the field before shooting. Other suggested photographs are the façade, close-ups of the typical window and main entrance, eaves and verges, and any other important detail. Every roll of film is assigned a sequential number by the recorder/photographer team which, in turn, is identified by a unique code. Developed negatives and duplicate contact prints are stored in photo ledgers at the office. The original 35 mm contact prints are cut and attached to the photo card by the recorder/photographer.

Tasks

Certain information is coded only by the office staff; most is answered and coded directly by the field recorders. Only office staff code the names of the architect(s), builder(s) or contractor(s), and engineer(s) each into five-digit codes. However, these questions, like the location information used for geocoding by office staff, are answered in text by field recorders. Office staff also mark the codes indicating the certainty with which dates and names are known as well as update any eventual data on demolition. Questions marked 'office use only' are answered uniquely by the headquarters staff: the recognized historic site, the style, the archaeological site, and the references. These are the last questions on the form.

Recording questions, answers and codes are fully described, defined and illustrated in the *Exterior Recording Training Manual*. Most computerized questions are directly answered by the recorder using the appropriate numeric code on the recording form. The printed division of the answer space prompts the recorder to write the correct number of digits. An unbroken line is provided for those questions answered in one digit; two divisions for two digits, etc. Correct answers are either written into the appropriate spaces or checked off.

The geocode

The nucleus of the CIHB system is the geocode, which is a unique number assigned by office staff to every building recorded. Fifteen digits code the building location. For urban Canada the province/territory, city, street (all coded) and number on the street are combined in a string of fourteen digits with the fifteenth representing any fraction or alpha letter used in the street address. In rural areas the province/territory, map number and number on the map are coded. Generally using standard 1:50,000 topographic maps, the CIHB assigns an individual number to each one used; each building recorded on that map is marked and identified with a number assigned in sequence as recorded.

Hierarchical codes

The several questions that consider use are all coded from one hierarchical list of more than 200 specific uses grouped into seventeen general uses. The four-digit use code combines the general use with the specific use. Thus the code 0104 represents residential use (01) and apartment building (04). It is possible to search for all buildings of the same general-use group (residential, religious, etc.) or only for a specific use (apartment building or monastery). Each of the seventeen general-use groups contain about ten precoded specific use possibilities as well as the term 'other' which is always precoded 99. This is used to code the specific use of a building when that use is not included in the precoded selections. When additional kinds of specific uses are discovered they may be assigned the next highest number in the numeric sequence within that general-use group and added to the open-ended list.

COMPUTERIZATION

Computerization of CIHB data is provided by the Department of Indian Affairs and Northern Development. Input costs are one dollar per entry. Total maintenance, storage, searching and output costs are C$45,000 per year. The programming language is COBOL; MARK IV is used for report generating. Record length is fixed at 640 spaces. All entries are in numeric code and data are stored as numerics. Output is in numeric codes or in either French or English keywords.

Data retrieval is fast and flexible. Searches can be run and indices printed, based on any question or answer, or combination of questions and answers. This applies whether one or all entries are being searched. An office CRT terminal is linked to the main data base via a telephone hook-up.

USERS AND PRODUCTS

Although primarily designed to provide data to enable the Historic Sites and Monuments Board to judge the significance of a building or groups of buildings by comparison with others having similar features and values, the inventory also serves as an accessible source of basic architectural data. Copies of the documented building reports are placed in the Public Archives of Canada and the various Provincial Archives. All recorded information is available to the public at cost. However, computer listings of a given area may be obtained without charge by those willing to verify recorded information and to suggest additional buildings that should be recorded.

Two primary products are the photographs of all recorded buildings and the computerized forms and indices. Secondary products include the information files compiled by office staff on early Canadian architects, builders and engineers as well as in-depth studies prepared on building types, materials and technology and the origin of Canadian building styles.

Summary/Evaluation

The objectives of the project have been surpassed. Originally designed for the Historic Sites and Monuments Board, the inventory has become a major resource for architectural research. Since 1970 the CIHB has been in operation as a computerized method to locate and record pre-1914 architecture. It is a proven, continuing system. Particular revisions over the years between the first edition (1970) and the present fourth edition (1979) are based on experience gained in recording and analysis. Bilingual in English and French, the descriptive manual and the illustrated selection form systematically teach a nomenclature of architecture which simplifies training of professional staff and quickly teaches volunteers 'to see a building' using its grid format.

Tasks are well defined for both field and office staff. The majority of questions are directly coded by the recorder and need not be recoded in the office, thereby saving time. Certainty codes for names and dates distinguish the accuracy level of the research. Emphasis is placed on the complete physical description of the building exterior, part by part, element by element. All entries are photographed on standard 35 mm black-and-white film. Resulting photo cards provide handy office reference. Predominantly precoded answers make the data easy to understand and to compare. Computerized indices can be printed out from any combination of questions and answers.

Nevertheless, there are problems. Photographic information is not computerized, so the photo card must be consulted in order to identify each negative roll and shot. Field selection of appropriate buildings is based on the recorders' variable understanding of the pre-1914 cut-off date and ability to locate such structures. No separate consistent map co-ordinate system is used for location in rural areas; in order to establish which property is recorded, a duplicate copy of the CIHB map sheet is needed. No free text entry is allowed. Owing to the large size of each entry and the great number of entries, it is extremely difficult to update computerized information, correct errors or make changes to data. No statistical package exists for data analysis. However, some of these disadvantages are being amended in present revisions to the computer program.

Question analysis

An analysis of the kinds of information asked by the CIHB follows. The analysis is by question category and not by the question sequence on the form. For a question-by-question comparison of these Canadian questions contrasted with the other systems see Part Three.

IDENTIFICATION/LOCATION

Urban location information is given by province/territory, town, street and building number. Rural buildings are identified by province/territory, map number and building number on the map. Both urban and rural locations are coded by office staff into the unique entry number or geocode at the top of the form. County, district and township are identified and computerized under Question 80. Concession and lot numbers are asked but not computerized.

The name or names of the building are asked but not computerized with the main data. They are computerized separately and cross-referenced to the location information. Two present uses (primary and secondary) and two original uses (primary and secondary) as well as up to five associated uses, from any time period, are recorded. If the original use was the same as the present use it is noted. The state of the present use (i.e. abandoned, vacant or occupied) is given.

SIGNIFICANCE/DESIGNATION

No question deals with the level of significance.

43

The first edition of the CIHB (1970) included levels of significance. The present fourth edition (1979) no longer records this since 'only the Historic Sites and Monuments Board can recommend to the Minister whether a building should be designated as a historic site'.

For those entries that have been officially designated four levels of recognized historic site are coded—national, provincial, regional or municipal.

DATE/HISTORY

The years during which construction was begun and completed are given in true numerics. For buildings destroyed after surveying, the numeric year is added when discovered. Accuracy of all dates is stated, whether known or estimated and this, in turn, is modified by certainty codes. 'A' represents non-staff research; 'R' represents staff research.

Three possibilities are allowed for each of the following: architect(s) builder(s) or constructor(s), and engineer(s). Their names are written in text by the recorder and numerically coded by office staff. Certainty codes also modify these names.

DESCRIPTION

Since structures moved from their original sites cannot be designated by the Historic Sites and Monuments Board one question determines this fact. Any property features such as gates, fences, are noted. Questions concerning dimension and volume include the actual depth and width of the structure in metres, number of bays, size of basement, number of storeys, massing, type of plan and if wings have been added to the plan. A style question is for office use only; up to three different styles can modify each entry.

Most building elements and parts are described: roof (type, special shapes, trims, special features); chimney (location, stacks); dormer types; towers, steeples and domes; main stairs (location and direction); main entrance (location, structural opening shape, trims); door (leaves, panels, special features); porch (type, special features, height); window (typical location, opening shape, trims, special types, special panes); wall design and details.

Exterior bearing-wall construction technique is determined as well as the materials of the main exterior wall, additional exterior walls, roof surface and trims, chimney stacks, windowsill and trims, entrance trims, and main porch.

CONSERVATION/RESTORATION/PRESERVATION

Apparent alterations and additions are noted.

DOCUMENTATION/REFERENCE

Maps are used to locate rural buildings. A separate Dominion land survey map may be listed but this is not computerized. The 'archaeological site' question indicates that some information is held in the separate files of the Archaeology Division. The 'reference' question identifies the fact that information may exist in separate CIHB files of reports, dossiers, plans and elevations, historical photographs, slides or interior information.

For each entry the total count of photographs taken, the photographer's name and film-roll number are requested but this information is not computerized. Black-and-white 35 mm contact prints are attached to the photo card.

The 'observation' question (not computerized) provides a space to include all pertinent data not coded, such as special details or drawings and any sources used to record the building.

SYSTEMATIZATION

Recording record
The full date of the survey is coded by day, month and year. Team number, and the names of the photographer and recorder are asked but not computerized.

Systematics
The geocode provide the unique identification number for each entry.

Appendix
ORIGINAL QUESTION SEQUENCE (FORM CA)

(Geocode)	(Géocode)
Province/territory	Province/territoire
Total No. of photos taken	Nombre total de photos
Film-roll No.	No. de la bobine du film
Town	Ville
Team number	No. de l'équipe
County	Comté
District	District
Township	Canton
Street	Rue
Map No.	No. de la carte
Building No.	No. du bâtiment
Concession No.	No. de la concession
Lot No.	No. du lot
Dominion land survey	Arpentage des terres fédérales
Present owner	Propriétaire actuel
Address of owner	Adresse du propriétaire
Tenant	Locataire
Original owner or tenant	Propriétaire ou locataire d'origine
Building name	Nom du bâtiment

	Recorder	Enquêteur
	Photographer	Photographe
1.	Year(s) of construction known or estimated (certainty code)	Année(s) de construction—données connues ou estimatives
2.	Year of demolition known or estimated (certainty code)	Année de démolition—données connues ou estimatives
3.	Architect (certainty code)	Architecte
4.	Major builder or contractor (certainty code)	Entrepreneur principal ou constructeur
5.	Engineer (certainty code)	Ingénieur
6.	Present use	Usage actuel
	Primary use	Usage principal
	Secondary use	Usage secondaire
7.	Original use (unknown/same)	Usage initial (inconnu/même)
	Primary use	Usage principal
	Secondary use	Usage secondaire
8.	Associate or other uses	Usages apparentés ou autres
9.	State	État
10.	Site	Emplacement
11.	Massing of units	Groupement des unités
12.	Plan	Plan
13.	Wings	Ailes
14.	Building dimension in metres	Dimensions du bâtiment en mètres
15.	Storeys	Étages
16.	Number of bays	Nombre de baies
17.	Basement/foundation	Sous-sol/fondations
18.	Basement/foundation wall material	Matériau des murs de fondation ou du sous-sol
19.	Main exterior wall material—earth	Matériau principal du mur extérieur—terre
20.	Wood	Bois
21.	Stone-shape and coursing	Pierre-forme et assise
22.	Stone-finish	Pierre-finition
23.	Brick-bond	Brique-appareil
24.	Composition	Matériau fabriqué
25.	Concrete	Béton
26.	Metal	Métal
27.	Glass	Verre
28.	Additional exterior wall	Autre matériau du mur extérieur
29.	Exterior wall material—other walls	Matériau des murs extérieurs—autres murs
30.	Exterior bearing wall construction	Construction des murs porteurs extérieurs
31.	Wall design and detail	Dessin et détail des murs
32.	Roof type	Type de toit
33.	Special shapes	Profiles spéciaux
34.	Roof surface material	Matériau de la surface du toit
35.	Roof trim—eaves	Garniture du toit—avant-toit
36.	Roof-trim material—eaves	Matériau de la garniture du toit—avant-toit
37.	Roof trim—verges	Garniture du toit—bordures
38.	Roof-trim material—verges	Matériau de la garniture du toit—bordures
39.	Towers, steeples and domes—types	Tours, clochers et dômes—types
40.	Towers, steeples and domes—location side to side	Emplacement des tours, clochers et dômes—position latérale
41.	Towers, steeples and domes—location front to rear	Emplacement des tours, clochers et dômes—avant-arrière
42.	Dormer type	Type de lucarne
43.	Chimney location—side to side	Emplacement de la cheminée—position latérale
44.	Chimney location front to rear	Emplacement de la cheminée—avant-arrière
45.	Chimney-stack material	Matériau des souches de cheminée
46.	Chimney-stack massing	Groupement des souches de cheminée
47.	Roof trim—special features	Garniture du toit—particularités
48.	Typical window—location	Fenêtre typique—emplacement
49.	Structural opening shape	Forme de l'ouverture structurale
50.	Trim outside structural opening—head	Garniture à l'extérieur de l'ouverture structurale—tête
51.	Trim outside structural opening—sides	Garniture à l'extérieur de l'ouverture structurale—côtés
52.	Trim outside structural opening—material	Garniture à l'extérieur de l'ouverture structurale—matériau
53.	Windowsill—type	Seuil de fenêtre—type
54.	Windowsill—material	Seuil de fenêtre—matériau
55.	Trim within structural opening—head	Garniture à l'intérieur de l'ouverture structurale—tête
56.	Trim within structural opening—sides	Garniture à l'intérieur de l'ouverture structurale—côtés
57.	Number of sashes	Nombre de châssis
58.	Opening mechanism	Mécanisme d'ouverture
59.	Special window types	Types particuliers de fenêtres
60.	Special pane arrangements	Disposition particulière des carreaux
61.	Main entrance location	Entrée principale—emplacement
62.	Structural opening shape	Forme de l'ouverture structurale
63.	Trim outside structural opening—head	Garniture à l'extérieur de l'ouverture structurale—tête

64. Trim outside structural opening—sides — Garniture à l'extérieur de l'ouverture structurale—côtés
65. Trim outside structural opening—material — Garniture à l'extérieur de l'ouverture structurale—matériau
66. Trim within structural opening—head — Garniture à l'intérieur de l'ouverture structurale—tête
67. Trim within structural opening—sides — Garniture à l'intérieur de l'ouverture structurale—côtés
68. Number of leaves — Nombre de vantaux
69. Number of panels per leaf — Nombre de panneaux par vantail
70. Leaves—special features — Vantaux—particularités
71. Main stairs—location and design — Escalier principal—emplacement et conception
72. Main stairs—direction — Escalier principal—direction
73. Main porch—type — Porche principal—type
74. Main porch—special features — Porche principal—particularités
75. Main porch—material — Porche principal—matériau
76. Main porch—height — Porche principal—hauteur
77. Apparent alterations and/or additions — Modifications et/ou rajouts apparents
78. Property features — Caractéristiques de la propriété
79. Date of survey — Date de l'enquête
80. Office use only — A l'usage du bureau seulement
81. Recognized historic site — Reconnu lieu historique
82. Style — Style
83. Archaeological site — Site archéologique
84. Reference — Référence

France (FR)

Inventaire Général des Monuments et des Richesses Artistiques de la France

Based on information supplied by
Michel Berthod, former *sous-directeur*,
and Marie-Claude Méplan, *chercheur*

Discussion

OBJECTIVES AND STATISTICS

The Inventaire Général des Monuments et des Richesses Artistiques de la France is one *sous-direction* for the Direction du Patrimoine of the Ministère de la Culture et de la Communication. The objectives of the Inventaire are systematically to inventory, research and publicize all works which, because of their artistic, historical, archaeological or ethnographic character, are part of the national heritage.

From the creation of the service in 1964, computerization of the documentation was planned in order to create national and regional documentation centres, and to publish *Indicateurs du Patrimoine* based on the standardized findings.

Architecture is one subject of investigation for the Inventaire, in addition to works of art and archaeology. For architecture, neither recording nor research is limited to buildings protected by law. The Inventaire points out buildings and structures that merit protection. It has, however, no legal power to protect buildings. This is the duty of the Service des Monuments Historiques which is another *sous-direction* of the Direction du Patrimoine.

The present computerized *Inventaire* methodology became operational in 1979. As at 31 December 1980, there was 24,000 entries in the architecture data base. It is anticipated that the architectural heritage of the whole of France will be recorded by the year 2010. The total Inventaire budget for 1980 was 13,507,000 francs ($3,374,000).

STAFF

Work is divided between Paris and regional services. The total staff for Paris and the regions was 186 at the beginning of 1981. Permanent personnel (recruited by competition) and contractual positions include: seventy-one curators (art historians or historians); fourteen scientific agents; forty technical agents (photographers, draftsmen and documentalists; twenty-one administrative agents; and forty part-time technical and administrative agents.

In addition, about 100 volunteers assist in the regions. The quality of their work varies. All volunteer assistance is reviewed by staff. No special training programme exists for volunteers.

CRITERIA

For the architectural inventory, exteriors of the entire built heritage are recorded. Works may be extant, destroyed, disappeared or unlocatable. Criteria are comprehensive enough to cover any built object cited in the *Cadastre Napoléonien* (1805–45)[1] and selective for more recent works. Works dated pre-400 are inventoried by the Service des Fouilles Archéologiques, another *sous-direction* of the same ministry.

Selection of recent works is made by the regional services according to their knowledge of the land. In order to obtain a representative national selection the first objective is to ensure a uniform coverage of the country. Within each canton the selection may be concentrated in one locality when structures throughout the canton are relatively homogeneous, or dispersed throughout the canton when heterogeneity is the case. Alternatively, selection may be distributed according to type. Thus, within a given region some selections may be of exceptional buildings; others of the most common type.

1. 1865–70 for Nice and Savoy only.

METHOD

The system combines a computerized index with in-depth descriptive dossiers containing supporting documentation. These descriptive dossiers are eventually microfiched. One form, the *bordereau architecture*, is used for computer entry. Questions and terms are described in the detailed manuals entitled *Vocabulaire de l'architecture* and *Lexique de la zone 1 pour l'architecture*. The standardized method and vocabulary allow regional work, yet guarantee homogeneity of the entries and their documentation.

Site visits are necessary for a building to be noted in the Inventaire. Within the limits of the selection criteria all constructions should be noted, but they cannot all be studied. Thus, two kinds of entry are made. The PIN (*pré-inventaire normalisé*) notes succinct identification and location information; the IF (*inventaire fondamental*) studies in depth.

The IF includes supporting dossiers of textual historical research, description and bibliography plus plans, drawings, photographs, and photogrammetry. All dossier documentation will eventually be on microfiche. Since the Inventaire predates the present system, dossiers may exist prior to computer entry. If a dossier does exist it provides the data for the entry. If no dossier exists the entry is first established as a PIN and updated if and when a dossier is established.

COMPUTERIZATION

Data processing is done at CIMAC, the data-processing centre of the Ministry of Culture and Communication. The software is MISTRAL which is written in Assembler (Honeywell-Bull CII); all auxiliary programs are written in PL/1. Entry length is open, but averages twenty lines of forty characters each. Entry is by keyword with some free text for commentary.

Some keyword lists are open-ended and can be added to as new keywords occur, as for example with the questions concerning denomination category and type, type of user, constituent parts, location, and materials. Questions answered in free text are the title of a work or its names, specifics of representation, historical commentary, authors' names and regional types.

The MISTRAL software provides a flexible indexing system. All computerized data are easily corrected, updated and expanded. With the aid of a terminal, and in conversational mode, the user can: (a) find a descriptive document or a work defined principally by its geographic characteristics; (b) select a subset of documents pertinent to a question posed in terms of keywords; (c) combine questions and eventually search free text. Simple commands ease access by non-computer people.

Computerized indices include: EDI CART, a general map of points in each commune of a canton; EDI FICH, a listing of all data on cards; and EDI CANT, a listing by cantons sorted by location and subject.

USERS AND PRODUCTS

The Inventaire is used by the various governmental services responsible for protection, conservation, restoration and the environment as well as researchers, archaeologists, historians and art historians. A series of documentation centres open to the general public are planned for Paris and the regions within three years. Each will have a set of all microfiches and be on-line for interrogation via telephone with the main data base located in Paris.

Products include computerized print-out listings such as EDI CART, EDI FICH, and EDI CANT and supporting documentation dossiers which contain textual historic research, descriptions and bibliography as well as photographs, photogrammetry, plans and maps. Eventually all supporting documentation will be on microfiches.

The Inventaire is mandated to sensitize the French public to their national heritage, an objective reached through expositions produced with survey materials. It also edits several series of publications which include all subjects of the Inventaire; architecture, archaeology, sculpture, paintings, objects, and furniture. Among these the *Indicateur du patrimoine* presents computerized findings in topographic order with maps and multiple indices. The *Inventaire topographique* cites every work studied within a canton or group of cantons and is abundantly illustrated. The *Repertoires des inventaires* provide analytic bibliography by region, by department and by category of works. An illustrated two-volume *Vocabulaire de l'architecture* has been published which is a scientific analysis and definition of architectural terms; additional *vocabulaires* for sculpture and tapestries have also been published. Other *vocabulaires* for objects, furniture and paintings will soon appear.

Summary/Evaluation

The Inventaire Général is an immense undertaking within a nationwide policy to inventory, research and publicize systematically the entire cultural heritage of France. For architecture all the built heritage, as known from the *Cadastre Napoléonien*, is to be recorded, plus recent works. Since all entries cannot be studied to the same degree, two types of entry are made. A *pré-inventaire normalisé* (PIN) notes all works within its broad selection criteria. The in-depth *inventaire fondamental* (IF) studies some selected works by means of supporting dossiers of historical research, description and bibliography plus plans, drawings, photographs and photogrammetry. All documentation is of the highest quality.

Microfiches provide a flexible means for reproducing the original texts of historical research, description and bibliography as well as the copious visual and graphic documentation. Duplicate microfiches will be available for general use and consultation in multiple documentation centres.

The computer index is easily updated and expanded. Once a preliminary (PIN) entry is made it can be expanded and enriched as new information is found. Storage of data as keywords and free text allows the system to be easily understood and interrogated. Hierarchical lists permit systematic searches. Cross-references to dossiers and microfiches are built into the computer form. Computerized indices such as EDI CART, EDI FICH, and EDI CANT or MIS-CART, MIS-FICH and MIS-CANT provide basic data for standard serial publications to publicize the work in the *Indicateur du patrimoine* or *Inventaire topographique*.

Nevertheless, the size and scope of the project necessitate at least thirty additional years for completion of the architectural registration. Although computerization has been planned since the creation of the service in 1964, the actual system was not operational until 1979. Documentation centres have always been an objective, but the first will only open three years from now. While the standardized method and vocabulary guarantee the homogeneity of the documentation, the actual regional selection of entries varies; some samples may be of exceptional buildings, others of the most common type.

Question analysis

The kind of information asked on the *bordereau architecture* is analysed below by category and not by the question sequence on the form. There are approximately forty questions. Not all questions, of course, are answered for each entry. For a question-by-question comparison of these French questions contrasted with the other systems, see Part Three.

IDENTIFICATION/LOCATION

The single French question '*dénomination*' combines two elements, the general category of entry and the specific type. Five of these general categories hierarchically divide 389 individual types. The categories are collectives, ensembles, buildings (*édifices*), constructions (*édicules*), and displaced parts (*parties*). Collectives comprise cantons, towns, and villages; ensembles are groupings; buildings are habitable spaces; constructions are non-habitable; displaced parts are architectural parts that have been moved from their original location.

Within '*dénomination*' the 389 individual types are arranged hierarchically. For example, within the buildings (*édifices*) category one finds *édifices religieux chrétiens* divided into church, convent, etc. Within each are further subdivisions—i.e. *église*, subdivided into *cathédrale*, *basilique*, *collégiale*.

Two other questions specify the denomination: the type of user (*genre du destinataire*); and the title(s) or name(s) of the building. Thus the full denomination is *édifice religieux chrétien—église*. The type of user is '*de Jésuites*'. The name of the church is '*Saint Louis*'. Present use is given. Regional types and constituent parts or uses not implied by the denomination term are also cited.

In order to locate the entry, the region, department, canton, commune, place-name or urban sector and address have to be stated. Street addresses are not necessary for churches, town halls, etc., but are indispensable for houses. Specifics of the address detail also non-locatable buildings, disappeared constructions, museum holdings of moved parts, as well as 'forbidden addresses' which modify works belonging to private owners who refuse public access to their address.

The most ancient as well as recent cadastral references are cited, including references for parts which have been moved. The appropriate Lambert zone and precise co-ordinates are stated. The Lambert projection divides France into four zones. For buildings, constructions and small groups the Lambert '*x-y*' co-ordinates define a point of reference in the approximate centre of the work. For large groups, ensembles, collectives, etc., the four corner co-ordinates of a superimposed rectangle are given. Such data allow maps to be automatically printed out by the computer.

Ownership of the entry is described in 'legal status'. The type of public or private ownership as well as museum storage for a moved part may be cited.

SIGNIFICANCE/DESIGNATION

The interest or significance of the work is signalled as 'protected', 'merits protection' or, for destroyed works 'would have merited protection'. Official designation is noted in 'legal status' which gives the date of any classification or inscription by the Monuments Historiques.

DATE/HISTORY

Dates may be written either in text to the nearest quarter century or in arabic numerals for exact years. The same question specifies whether the date is known by research, date-stone, etc. Historical commentary describes building campaigns and any inscriptions, monograms, or mason's marks. Authors are named—the *maître d'œuvre*, any painters and sculptors associated with the work—as well as how they are identified, by signature, attribution, etc.

DESCRIPTION

The immediate setting or placement of the entry can be isolated, or in a cluster, village or city. If it has been reused from, or moved to, another location this is stated. For collective forms that provide information on several buildings or constructions the count is given.

Only the dimensions of constructions (not buildings) are determined. For buildings the exterior elevation, number of floors, and plan type can all be detailed. The types of roof, vault and stairways are described. Decorative techniques are stated as are the materials of both the roof and the total work. Some works of art located either within or on the architectural work may not merit separate entries as sculpture or painting. For these the type of subject represented is noted and the particular specific given in free text.

CONSERVATION/RESTORATION/PRESERVATION

Only the present state of conservation is detailed; it may be destroyed, destroyed after recording, ruins, *mauvais état*, *menacé* or restored. If the condition is good the question is not answered.

DOCUMENTATION/REFERENCE

If the *bordereau* is completed from a dossier, this is stated under 'documentation reference'. If the dossier contains either measured drawings or photogrammetry, these are separately noted. Cross-reference is made to the photographic and text microfiche numbers.

SYSTEMATIZATION
Recording record

Not asked on the *bordereau* but entered into the computer is the date of the survey.

Systematics

Every entry is assigned a unique machine number. Each text or photo microfiche is numbered, as well as any continuation micro-fiche.

Appendix

ORIGINAL QUESTION SEQUENCE
AND TRANSLATION (FORM FR)

Bordereau architecture		*Architecture form*
1000	No. machine	Machine number
5	Documentation, référence	Documentation reference
1010	Dénomination	Denomination
1030	Genre du destinataire	Type of user
10	Titres—appellations, etc. Destination actuelle, etc.	Titles—names of structures, etc. Present use, etc.
1060	Parties constituantes	Constituent parts
1070	Représentation	Representation
20	Précisions, etc.	Specifics, etc.
1130	Région No. du département Canton Commune	Region Department number Canton Commune
30	Lieu-dit ou secteur urbain	Place or urban sector
40	Adresse, etc.	Address
1140	Précisions sur localisation	Specifics
50	Références cadastrales Edifice ou ensemble de conservation	Cadastral reference Displaced conserved parts
1170	Coordonnées cartographiques	Cartographic coordinates
1210	Milieu d'implantation	Placement
1250	Remplois	Reuse
1260	Déplacement	Displacement
1310	Auteurs	Authors
1320	Origine de l'identification	Identification
1370	Datation	Dating
60	Commentaire historique	Historical commentary
1390	Matériau de gros œuvre	Material of total structure
1400	Matériau de couverture	Material of roofing
1410	Importance du bordereau collectif	Importance for collective form
1420	Plan	Plan
1430	Vaisseaux et étages	Naves and floors
1450	Technique de décoration	Decoration technique
1460	Parti d'élévation extérieure	Exterior elevation
1470	Type de couverture	Roof type
1480	Type de couvrement	Vault type
1490	Dimensions	Dimensions

1500	Type d'escalier	Stairways type
70	Typologie régionale	Regional typology
1510	Conservation	Conservation
1550	Situation juridique	Legal status
1590	À signaler: intérêt de l'œuvre	Interest in the work
80	Mise à jour de la microfiche	Continuation

India (IN)

Record of Protected Monuments and Sites

Based on information supplied by
K. M. Srivastava, Director (Monuments)

Discussion

OBJECTIVES

The Record of Protected Monuments and Sites is maintained by the Archaeological Survey of India, which was begun in 1904. The record serves as a guide for the administration and conservation of those monuments and sites that have been centrally protected.

Forms are completed in duplicate in each regional circle office by staff. One copy with attachments is sent to the Director General of the Archaeological Survey in New Delhi where central files are maintained for the whole of the country.

CRITERIA

All monuments and sites in the record are of national importance and have been centrally protected. Copies of the legal notifications are attached to each entry. However, the record is maintained for official use and has no legal status as such.

METHOD

Information is recorded in English on two forms. Form A, Record of Protected Monuments and Sites, is a fold-out format of eight sides, twenty-five questions. Most of these questions are answered in text paragraphs. Copies of legal documents, photographs, and drawings are attached. The List of Centrally Protected Monuments and Sites of National Importance is a shorter form for administrative purposes. This asks nine questions which are generally answered in one word or a brief statement.

PRODUCTS AND USERS

The products of the Indian system are the List of Centrally Protected Monuments and Sites of National Importance and the central collection of forms and attachments arranged by state, which comprise the Record of Protected Monuments and Sites.

These manual files are used by the staff personnel of the Archaeological Survey of India as a guide to the administration and conservation of the sites. Copies of the completed forms for the region are kept in each circle office; copies of the completed forms with enclosures are collected in the central office in New Delhi.

Summary/Evaluation

Used manually, the Record of Protected Monuments and Sites provides a permanent dossier of information in English for all centrally protected monuments and sites. Copies of all legal notifications for each entry as well as photographs and drawings are attached. Question emphasis is on information relevant to the administration and conservation of the entries. In particular, for administration, the approach is detailed. This includes the nearest railway station and authority for reservation of accommodation to facilitate future site inspections. Staff associated with the monument or site are identified. Two questions discuss conservation. Climatic data give information on temperature and rainfall useful for planning furture conservation. Outstanding structural and chemical conservation work undertaken in the past are described.

Unfortunately, no handbook or lexicon exists for the system. Few directions or clarifications are stated on the forms. The fold-out format for the record is unwieldy. Long paragraphs of text are difficult to read and to compare. Some answer paragraphs may combine several topics worthy of point-by-point discussion rather than generalization. For example, Question 6: 'Brief history, importance and outstanding features of the monument including references to sculpture, paintings, inscriptions.' This single complex question mixes far too much. History, importance, description and particular features each warrant a separate shorter answer.

Question analysis

An analysis of the kinds of information asked on the record and list follows. Analysis is by category and not by the question sequence on the forms. For a question-by-question comparison of these Indian questions contrasted with the other systems, see Part Three.

INDENTIFICATION/LOCATION

Both forms ask the name of the monument/site, district and locality. The record includes the name of the Indian state as well as alternative names for the monument. The subdivision, revenue circle, post office, police station and *tehsil/talik* (tax district) can all be specified. One question, Approach, details the nearest railway station, transport and halting facility as well as authority for accommodation reservation. North latitude and east longitude co-ordinates provide specific geographic references; the number of the appropriate one-inch survey sheet is stated.

The shorter list asks whether the entry is used for religious purposes; the record details utilization. Both discuss ownership. In the case of government ownership the record form asks if the monument or site was a gift or bequest. If so, the section and act are quoted and a copy of the 'instrument' is attached. The name of the responsible agency is also given.

SIGNIFICANCE/DESIGNATION

All entries are recorded because they have been centrally protected. On the record one complex question details importance as well as brief history and outstanding features.

Precise legal protection (notification) is spelled out. Both forms specify the number and date of notification. The record also asks for the authority, and section and act under which the monument or site is protected. Full copies of the official notifications are typed on the record. Any revenue from an endowment or lease is noted. Both forms specify if any agreement exists between the government lent and the owner. If one does exist, the record also states the section and act and copies are attached.

DATE/HISTORY

One complex question on the record includes brief history as well as outstanding features and importance.

DESCRIPTION

On the record the legal area and boundary are cited. Separate questions discuss topographical features of the site as well as the nature and extent of any garden attached to the monument. Further horticultural notes may be referenced in the question describing office files. Staff attached to the monument are identified.

Outstanding features such as sculpture, paintings and inscriptions are mentioned in the question which also includes brief history and importance. Additional epigraphic notes may be referenced in the office files question.

CONSERVATION/RESTORATION/PRESERVATION

Several questions on the longer record relate to conservation. Climatic data provide information on temperature and rainfall for planning future conservation. Outstanding structural and chemical conservation thus far carried out are described. Further conservation notes and inspection notes may be referenced in the question on the office files.

DOCUMENTATION/REFERENCE

Published references include bibliographic citations from imperial and district gazetteers, and local manuals as well as from selected sources. The question concerning office files may reference horticultural, epigraphic, conservation, inspection and administrative notes. Photographs and drawings held in the circle office are mentioned in separate questions. Selected photographs and sketches are pasted on sheets to be attached to the record. Both forms have questions called remarks which allow for 'unknown whatevers' to be recorded.

SYSTEMATIZATION

Recording record
The superintendent of the circle office that completed the forms signs and dates it.

Systematics
The shorter list assigns a serial number to each entry within every state.

Appendix

ORIGINAL QUESTION SEQUENCE
(FORM IN1)

Record of protected monuments and sites

State

District

1. Name of monument/site...
2. Locality
3. Latitude N. Longitude E.
   Survey sheet number
4. Sub-division, etc.
5. Approach
6. Brief history, importance and
   outstanding features, etc.
7. Published references, etc
8. Topographical features
9. Climatic data
10. Authority, number and date
    of notifications
11. Section and act under which protected
12. Ownership, etc.
13. Agreement, etc.
14. Utilization, etc.
15. Revenue, etc.
16. Area and boundary, etc.
17. Recorded classification
18. Office files
19. Structural and chemical conservation, etc.
20. Nature and extent of garden, etc.
21. Staff, etc.
22. Photographs, etc.
23. Drawings, etc.
24. Remarks
25. Superintendent's signature
    and date
    Copies of notifications

ORIGINAL QUESTION SEQUENCE
(FORM IN2)

*List of centrally protected
monuments and sites of national
importance*

1. Serial no.
2. District
3. Locality
4. Name of monument/site
5. Ownership
6. Used for religious purposes
7. Agreement
8. Authority, number and date
   of notification
9. Remarks

Italy (IT)

Catalogo dei Beni Culturali

Based on information provided by
Oreste Ferrari, Director, Istituto Centrale per il
Catalogo e la Documentazione (ICCD)

Discussion

OBJECTIVES AND STATISTICS

The Istituto Centrale per il Catalogo e la Documentazione (ICCD), created in 1969, is a facility of the Ministerio per il Beni Culturali e Ambientali. The Istituto serves as the central archive for the Catalogo dei Beni Culturali. The objectives of the Catalogo are to identify, research and document every cultural artefact of archaeological, art-historical, architectural, urbanistic, environmental or ethnographic interest.

The essential components of the Catalogo are: (a) a quantity and variety of artefacts to be catalogued which need to be identified, documented and researched within the framework of a specific category and within local cultural traditions; (b) a standard information system which is flexible, comprehensive and adaptable in order to provide basic data while accommodating in-depth research; and (c) an operative method which responds to the varied resources available in each region.

The Catalogo is not a static archive but is conceived as an 'anagraph'—a living body of information that continues to add new data. It records not only the object in its present state, but also changes and the events that bear upon them. The Catalogo is not considered as the sum of all the forms; it is rather the total findings that give the individual forms meaning.

The budget for the ICCD is 280 million lire ($280,000); the budget for all survey activity is 3,000 million lire ($3 million). Organization of documentation for movable objects began in 1969/70 and for monuments and other non-movable artefacts in 1974. The final total of entries cannot be foreseen. Between 120,000 and 130,000 entries in all categories are made each year.

STAFF

Surveys are carried out by *soprintendenze* within the Ministrio per il Beni Culturali or the Ministerio della Pubblica Istruzione as well as by separate institutes which record for the Catalogo according to the methodological directives of the ICCD. These agencies operate with variable levels of critical knowledge and resources within each region. Information is collected on separate forms for each category of entry. Two copies are made. One remains in the department; the other goes to the ICCD.

All data are compiled by the ICCD. A staff of forty-four includes three art historians, four archaeologists, three architects, five draughts-men-surveyors, nineteen photographers, five technical assistants, and five clerks. In addition, about 1,000 volunteers (art historians, archaeologists, draughtsmen, photographers) work on individual assignments.

CRITERIA

The Catalogo dei Beni Culturali is comprehensive. Free of any bias of a selective nature, it does not allow the entry of this or that type of cultural artefact corresponding to this or that chronological period found in this or that present condition to be biased by selective or subjective opinion.

Immovable and movable objects are divided into twenty-seven categories. Each category has its own entry form; many forms have additional inserts. For immovable objects various forms cover archaeology, architecture, parks and gardens, extra urban sectors, urban sectors, historic centres, and territories. For architecture, both legally protected and non-protected buildings are recorded. The form for architecture (Scheda A) and the three forms for an urban sector (Scheda SU) will be discussed in the Question Analysis.

METHOD

Forms

All forms are published in the *Repertorio delle schede di catalogo dei beni culturali*. Directives have been published in two manuals. One covers immovable objects, the other artistic and historical works; *Norme per la redazione delle schede di catalogo dei beni culturali, beni immobile* and ... *beni artistici e storici.*

Originally published in 1972, the present directives have been revised to deal with specific aspects of the cultural heritage in order to define the method better. Separate instructions are given for each form and insert. Although the questions are unnumbered on the forms the instructions are numbered.

All basic forms are of a standard size 52.6 × 30.5 cm open, 22.8 × 30.5 cm folded. Basic data are given first, followed by documentation references, historical-critical commentaries and conservation status. Supporting visual documentation is enclosed within the folded form.

COMPUTERIZATION

The Catalogo dei Beni Culturali is manual at present. Computerization, using thesauri of keywords in a natural language, is under development with the co-operation of CNUCE, an institute of the CNR, which specializes in computer research.

Basic data will be computerized corresponding to international standards for museum documentation such as those established by CIDOC (Comité International de Documentation) of ICOM.

USERS AND PRODUCTS

Primary products of the Catalogo include the completed standardized recording forms, photographic/graphic documentation, indices, topographic catalogues and a series of dictionaries. This series, under the general title 'Dizionari Terminologici' (Dictionaries of Terms) is intended to produce historical lexicons. A volume covering the archaeological materials from the last Bronze Age to the first Iron Age has appeared: *Materiali dell'età del bronze e della prima età del ferro.*

Users include state agencies for the administration of cultural heritage and public administration to whom various types of data are furnished by the Istituto Centrale; local and regional governments; police forces and customs agents in order to prevent illegal exports and recover cultural artefacts; cultural promotion agencies which organize exhibits, conventions and congresses, and scholars engaged in scientific research.

Summary/Evaluation

The objective of the Italian Catalogo dei Beni Culturali, to identify, research and document every cultural artefact of archaeological, art-historical, architectural, urbanistic, environmental or ethonographic interest, is extremely ambitious.

The ICCD provides the central archive for all forms and documentation as well as the methodological organization and co-ordination. Recording is done regionally by various agencies and departments as well as separate institutes.

All information is comprehensive and factual. Formats are standardized. Published standards (*norme*) describe the forms. Questions generally progress from basic to more complex. Information is recorded in a combination of short statements and longer paragraphs. Photographs and measured drawings are enclosed within the form for a complete visual record. The Catalogo is designed to be on-going; data can be updated.

The work, unfortunately, is done at different speeds and at various levels of critical knowledge and resources by the recording agencies. No evaluation is made of the importance of any entry; all are presumed to have equal significance. There are so many forms—twenty-seven plus insertions—that archive management, storage and retrieval of specific information could become unwieldy. On each form so much information is given that specific items are difficult to find. Long paragraphs of text often conceal important details. The shorter-answer statements, however, are easier to read and compare. These will lend themselves to computerization which is still under development.

Question analysis

An analysis follows of the kind of information asked on the forms for architecture (Scheda A) and for an urban sector (Scheda SU). The architecture form is used to record buildings or complexes of architectural, historical or monumental interest. The urban sector form is for small urban areas (*isolato*) delimited by four streets. Two separate inserts describe historic research (*indagine storica*) and present condition (*stato attuale*) for the sector. The analysis is by category and not by question sequence on the forms. For a question-by-question comparison of these Italian questions as contrasted with the other systems, see Part Three.

IDENTIFICATION/LOCATION

The region is given in the standard heading. Commune and province are stated using the

Automobile Club abbreviation for province. For architecture, the actual address is cited. For the urban sector, neighbourhood as well as streets delimiting the block are identified.

Both forms ask for cadastral references including folio, parcel and numbers. Precise topographic co-ordinates are given for the urban sector. Inserts describing historic research and present condition give the parcel number and organize all questions by it.

For architecture one question identifies the kind of object (oggetto) as well as the present and past names. Original uses and actual uses are given separately. 'None' for actual uses describes abandoned or unused buildings. Building types and distribution within the urban sector are noted. For each parcel the historic research insert gives past uses and the present condition insert states both present typology and use.

The architecture form gives the present owner by name and type. The urban sector inserts give the type of past or present owner for each parcel.

SIGNIFICANCE/DESIGNATION

No question deals with significance. On both architecture and urban sector forms the legal protection decrees (vincoli) are cited by number and date. Both protected and non-protected buildings are recorded.

DATE/HISTORY

Under 'chronology' both the architecture and urban sector forms give the century in roman numerals and the years in arabic numerals. The Historic Research Insert specifies the period for each parcel's historic information.

Construction events for architecture are stated in one question. A separate question describes urban events relative to the building's history. The historic research insert cites any historic events for each parcel; the present condition insert describes its development phases.

Author or architect is given only for architecture. Attributions are noted and multiple names in chronological sequence.

DESCRIPTION

On the architecture form a paragraph describes the urban setting surrounding the building. For the urban sector the present functional relationship to the rest of the city is described. In addition, successive changes in place-names, functions and division of land as well as volumetric relationships between open and built-up areas are given.

The question 'descrizione' on the architecture form combines levels, sizes and descriptions of the street façade. Separate questions specify the plan type as well as giving the materials and construction techniques of the roof, vaulting, exterior stairways, walls, flooring, exterior decoration, interior decoration, furnishings and subterranean structure. The present condition insert briefly notes construction technique.

On the architecture form one question identifies any inscriptions, tablets, coats of arms, and murals. Since the Italian Catalogo dei Beni Culturali records on individual forms all important works of art, the question 'elements of specific interest' (elementi di specifico interesse) notes within each urban sector those works which merit their own forms.

CONSERVATION/RESTORATION/PRESERVATION

Both old and more recent restorations for architecture are listed by date and type. In a separate grid format the conservation status (stato de conservazione) codes on a six-point scale walls, roof, attic, plaster and fixtures. The six possibilities are excellent (ottimo), good (buono), mediocre, bad (cattivo), very bad (pessimo) and ruined (rudere). Also the date of the conservation inspection is noted. Any specific damage and its causes are mentioned as observations.

On the urban sector present condition insert the conservation status is coded for subterranean, vertical and horizontal structures, roof and walls. Neither observations nor date are given.

DOCUMENTATION/REFERENCE

On both forms bibliography is given in chronological sequence with complete citations. Both formats also cross-reference any documentation enclosed within the file folder, such as the cadastral map extract, unspecified documents, photographs with negative numbers and dates, and measured drawings. Both completely reference additional non-held photographs citing negative numbers and source.

The architecture form also references maps, plans, measured drawings, engravings and technical reports; the urban sector form notes assembled plans, profiles, photographs of historic plans, aerial photos and extracts from historic centre documentation (straclio di parte de centro storico). The historical research insert specifies the document from which research was taken and its date.

Both the architecture and urban sector forms also reference information in separate archives. The question 'other forms' (altre schede) cross-references forms covering other categories within the Catalogo, as for example a mural that is the object of its own form. The urban sector form separately references the inserts by their titles. A subgroup number identifies each form of the same category related to the entry, i.e. each chapel of a church. This also can relate the urban sector to a large historical centre.

SYSTEMATIZATION

Recording record

The responsible ministry and the department which compiled the form along with that department's code number appear on the heading of the form. At the bottom of the form are the compiler's name and date, signature of approval for the department, reviser and date of revision.

Systematics

A unique identifier for each entry is derived from the alphabetical abbreviation for the form category plus the ten-digit catalogue number. The catalogue number is assigned by the ICCD. It codes the region in two digits followed by eight digits for the sequential number of the entry within the region. A blank space prefaced with 'ITA' is reserved for any future international catalogue number.

Appendix
ORIGINAL QUESTION SEQUENCE
AND TRANSLATION (FORM IT1)

A	Architecture form
N. catalogo generale	Catalogue general number
N. catalogo internazionale	International catalogue number
Ministerio	Ministry
Soprintendenza	Department and number
Regione	Region
N.	Subgroup number
Provincia e commune	Province and commune
Luogo	Address
Oggetto	Object
Catasto	Cadastre
Cronologia	Date
Autore	Author
Dest. originaria	Original use
Uso attuale	Present use
Proprieta	Ownership
Vincoli	Decrees
Tipologia edilizia—caratteri costruttivi:	Building typology—construction characteristics:
Pianta	Plan
Coperture	Roof
Volte—solai	Vault—attic
Scale	Stairs
Techniche murarie	Wall construction
Pavimenti	Flooring
Decorazioni esterne	Exterior decoration
Decorazioni interne	Interior decoration
Arredamenti	Furnishings
Strutture sotterranee	Subterranean structure
Descrizione	Description

Vicende Costruttive	Construction events
Sistema urbano	Urban system
Rapporti ambientai	Ambience
Iscrizioni—lapidi—stemmi—graffiti	Inscriptions, tablets, coats of arms, murals
Restauri	Restorations
Bibliografia	Bibliography
Stato di conservazione	Conservation status
Allegati:	Enclosed:
Estratto mappa cataste	Extract from cadastral map
Fotografie	Photographs
Disegni e rilievi	Plans and drawings
Mappe	Maps
Documenti vari	Other documents
Relazione tecniche	Technical reports
Riferimenti alle font. doc.:	Other documentation sources.
Fotografie	Photographs
Mappe—rilievi—stampe	Maps, plans, engravings
Archivi	Archives
Altre schede	Other forms
Compilatore della scheda	Compiler
Data	Date
Visto del soprintendente	Approved by
Revisioni	Revisions

ORIGINAL QUESTION SEQUENCE
AND TRANSLATION (FORM IT2)

SU	Urban sector form
N. catalogo generale	Catalogue general number
N. catalogo internazionale	International catalogue number
Ministerio	Ministry
Soprintendenza	Department and number
Regione	Region
N.	Sector number
Provincia e comune	Province and commune
Rione	Neighbourhood
Riferimenti topografici	Topographic coordinates
Vie di delimitazione	Delimiting streets
Catasto folio n. part. nm.	Cadastre folio parcel
Cronologia	Chronology
Vincoli	Decrees
Descrizione stato attuale:	Description of present state:
Correlazione urbanistiche par funzionali	Urban relationships by function
Individuazione dei tipi edilizi ed analisi della loro distribuzione	Building types and distribution
Vicende storico-critiche e construttive:	Historic and constructive events:
Etimologia della toponomastica	Etymology of place names
Impianto urbanistico originario	Original urban plant
Lottizzazione de impianto	Division of land

Correlazioni urbanistiche	Urbanistic relationship (of volumes)
Riferimento alle fonti doc.:	Other documentation sources:
Archivi	Archives
Iconografia	Iconography
Bibliografia	Bibliography
Fotografie	Photography
Allegati:	Enclosed:
Straclio di parte de Centro Storico	Extract from Centro Storico
Mappa catastale	Cadastral map
Planimetrie, etc.	Planimetry
Profili	Profiles
Fotografie di piante storiche	Photography of historic plans
Fotografie aeree	Aerial photography
Documenti vari	Other documents
Repertorio relativo, etc.	Inserts
Data	Date
Compilatore della scheda	Compiler
Revisione e aggiornamenti	Revisions and additions
Altre schede	Other forms
Visto del soprintendente	Approved by

ORIGINAL QUESTION SEQUENCE
AND TRANSLATION (FORM IT3)

SU	*Urban sector form*
Indagine storica	*Historical research insert*
N. catalogo generale	Catalogue general number
N. catalogo inter-nazionale	International catalogue number
Ministerio	Ministry
Soprintendenza	Department and number
Regione	Region
N.	Sector number
Allegato n.	Enclosure number

Provincia e comune	Province and commune
Compreso tra via	Delimiting streets
Catasto f.n.	Cadastre folio number
Particella	Parcel
Epoca	Period
Vicende storiche	Historic events
Proprieta	Ownership
Destinazioni	(Past) uses
Fonti	Sources
Documenti	Documents
Dati individuativi	Dates
Altre schede	Other forms

ORIGINAL QUESTION SEQUENCE
AND TRANSLATION (FORM IT4)

SU	*Urban sector*
Stato attuale	*Present condition insert*
N. catalogo generale	Catalogue general number
N. catalogo inter-nazionale	International catalogue number
Ministerio	Ministry
Soprintendenza	Department and number
Regione	Region
N.	Sector number
Allegato n.	Enclosure number
Provincia e comune	Province and commune
Compreso tra via	Delimiting streets
Catasto f.n.	Cadastre folio number
Particella	Parcel
Tipologia	Typology
Fasi di sviluppo	Development phases
Tecniche costruttive	Construction technique
Elementi di specifico interesse	Elements of special interest
Destinazioni d'uso	Use
Proprieta	Ownership
Stato di conservazione	Conservation status

Japan (JP)

Ledger of Designated Cultural Property

Based on information supplied by
Nobuto Ito, Director General, Tokyo National
Research Institute of Cultural Properties

Discussion

OBJECTIVES AND STATISTICS

The Japanese Ledger of Designated Cultural Property provides detailed descriptions of all cultural properties (tangible and intangible) officially designated by the state. Within the system three individual ledgers register immovable cultural property:

1. The Ledger of National Treasures and/or Important Cultural Properties (architecture) (treasures);
2. The Ledger of Historic Sites, Places of Scenic Beauty and/or Natural Monuments (sites);
3. The Ledger of Important Preservation Districts for Groups of Historic Buildings (districts).

A separate Record of Investigation on Archaeological and Historic Sites is compiled for sites with non-excavated cultural property. Although non-designated, the use of these sites is restricted by law.

The purpose of designation is 'to preserve and utilize cultural properties so that the culture of the Japanese people may be furthered and a contribution be made to the evolution of world culture'.

Designation is the first step for protection. Designation decisions result from individual studies of cultural properties prepared by local authorities or scholars.

The Record of Investigation on Archaeological and Historic Sites provides a map and card index of all sites with non-excavated remains within each prefecture. Excavation or disposal of these sites and objects found thereon are restricted by law.

The record, begun in 1960, contains more than 200,000 entries as of 31 December 1980. The Ledger of National Treasures, begun in 1897, has 3,096; the Ledger of Historic Sites (1919) has 2,294; the Ledger of Important Preservation Districts (1976) has fifteen.

STAFF

The ledgers are maintained by the Architecture and Monuments Divisions of the Agency for Cultural Affairs where technical specialists such as architects, archaeologists and historians collaborate. The Treasures and Districts Ledgers are both maintained by the staff of the Architecture Division. Two people are directly responsible for this function. The staff of the Monuments Division maintains the sites ledger and supervises the record, prepared in various card formats by each local prefecture.

Subsidized and supervised by the Architecture Division, local scholars and groups prepare Reports on the Emergency Investigations of Property. Structures listed in such reports are not protected by law, although the reports provide basic material for designation. The Report on the Emergency Investigation of Vernacular Buildings, completed in 1966, lists the exteriors and interiors of some 5,000 buildings. The Report on the Emergency Investigation of Modern [seventeenth- to nineteenth-century] Temples and Shrines, begun in 1977, is still continuing. Upon completion, some 13,000 building exteriors and interiors will have been investigated.

CRITERIA

The overall Ledger of Designated Cultural Property describes all cultural properties officially designated by the state. Besides tangible cultural properties and monuments it includes intangible cultural properties such as 'art and skill employed in drama, music and applied arts which possess a high historical and or artistic value' and folk cultural properties such as 'manners and customs . . . implements, houses and other objects . . . which are indispensable for the understanding of changes in . . . modes of life'.

Of the three particular ledgers that register immovable cultural property, that for National Treasures and/or Important Cultural Properties (architecture) includes building exteriors and interiors. Those of especially high value are designated national treasures. The Ledger of Historic Sites, Places of Scenic Beauty and/or Natural Monuments also lists archaeological sites, monumental dwelling houses, gardens, animals, plants and minerals. The Ledger of Important Preservation Districts covers building exteriors and their environments.

METHOD
The record

Each prefecture uses a different card format for the Record of Investigation on Archaeological and Historic Sites. Information is collected by local groups under the subsidy and supervision of the Monuments Division of the Agency for Cultural Affairs. Questions are limited to one side of a file card with a map and sketch plan or photograph of the site attached to the reverse. At present the record contains 200,000 entries for the whole of Japan; it will be revised in two or three years' time.

The ledgers

No lexicon or manual exists for the system. All questions are in Japanese and unnumbered. Although the formats for each ledger differ, topics concerning each are specified in rules established by the Commissioner of the Agency for Cultural Affairs.

There is no standardization in either size or questions. The National Treasures format asks approximately fourteen unnumbered questions. All are answered on one side of a sheet; there is a blank supplementary sheet. The Historic Sites format asks approximately thirty-five questions; half are answered on a grid. The Preservation District format asks approximately thirty unnumbered questions on eight sides of four pages. One side is used only for districts proposed for selection by the municipality.

PRODUCTS AND USERS

The individual ledgers for each of the particular types of designated cultural property as well as the attached maps, photographs and other supporting documentation are primary products of the system. Other products include the Reports on Emergency Investigations of Cultural Property and the Record of Investigation on Archaeological and Historic Sites.

The ledgers are mainly used for official administrative purposes by the Agency for Cultural Affairs and local officials, but also provide basic material for publication. The reports may be used as a basis for eventual designation. The record is used by the general public wishing to know, for construction or excavation projects, which archaeological and historic sites within each prefecture have non-excavated remains.

Summary/Evaluation

The Japanese Ledger of Designated Cultural Property continues a long tradition begun in 1897. Each separate ledger provides a permanent official record of all designated entries which are legally protected by the state. Photographs, drawings and maps are attached.

Prepared by the staff of the Agency for Cultural Affairs at the time of designation the ledgers have been continuously updated as new entries were designated. Recorded information varies according to the subjects covered in each ledger and thus reflects an evolution of the methodology since its origin.

All the data are objective and factual. Each ledger emphasizes the actual legal acts of designation rather than the complete physical description of the entry. In particular, the Ledger of Important Preservation Districts lists all possible legal acts, alterations and rules which might effect the entry. Only the Ledger of National Treasures includes information on date, history and physical description.

Unfortunately, no handbook or lexicon exists for the method. The various ledger formats are not unified. No cross-referencing exists among the ledgers, although some entries are designated in more than one. For example, monumental dwelling houses, i.e. 'the houses where great men were born', can be under 'historic sites' and at the same time under 'important cultural property'. The numeric quantity of ledger and record entries is straining the limits of the manual system.

Question analysis

An analysis follows of the kinds of information (translated into English) asked by the Ledger of National Treasures (treasures), the Ledger of Historic Sites (sites), and the Ledger of Important Preservation Districts (districts). Analysis is by category of question and not by question sequence on the ledger formats. For a question-by-question comparison of these Japanese questions contrasted with the other systems see Part Three.

IDENTIFICATION/LOCATION

All formats name the entry and its location for

which only city, town or village is indicated. Both the sites and districts formats give the numbers of the lots or range.

To determine use or type the treasures format asks for the structure and the sites format notes kind.

For ownership, the treasures format provides name and address of owner. For sites, the name and address of the owner or possessor is given for each lot.

SIGNIFICANCE/DESIGNATION

All the Japanese formats considered here devote considerable attention to this category, although with different emphasis on each of the three. For districts the term 'selection' rather than 'designation' is used. All formats provide the date of designation; in addition, the number of the certificate of designation is cited for treasures. Both sites and districts give the number of the announcement in the *Official Gazette*. For districts, a copy of the announcement is attached. Both sites and districts note the particular causes of designation or criteria for selection and provide an explanation of these. For sites, the actual paragraph and the item of legal criteria is referenced.

Both sites and districts also provide for the date of any alteration or changes to the official designation while districts further asks for the number of the alteration announcement in the *Official Gazette* and provides for two possible alteration citations.

For those preservation districts proposed for selection by the municipalities it is noted whether the area is within or outside a city planning district as well as the legal regulation for preservation. Further legal references for districts include related regulations and rules as well as the preservation plan. All are cited by name, date and number of announcement. An outline of the contents of the preservation plan is also provided. Date of establishment, date of enforcement and date of alteration further modify the regulation for preservation. Contents of legal measures taken by the municipality following selection are also stated.

DATE/HISTORY

Only the treasures format asks for the year or period of construction. Original construction and history are considered in a separate question.

DESCRIPTION

For treasures, the number of buildings is counted. For sites, the name of the custodian is specified. A grid gives the total area of land, total number of lots as well as the lots and acreage in both governmental and private possession, land category and section. For districts, the size of the area, population, number of households, houses and buildings are all detailed. For any alterations to the selection, the size of the area and range of lots are noted.

Only the treasures format provides a physical description of the entry. One general question combines structure, style, area, height and other details that indicate dimension. Another question discusses any tablet, inscription and other such items.

CONSERVATION/RESTORATION/PRESERVATION

Both the sites and districts formats deal with 'requisites for conservation', including the present condition of the entry and any necessary work.

DOCUMENTATION/REFERENCE

For treasures, both drawings and photographs are physically attached to the ledger and specific reference is made to the total count of drawings and photos. The sites format attaches drawings, prints, and photographs and their total count is noted. Cross-reference is made to the photo ledger number. Other reports are also cross-referenced. For districts, although a survey map, photos and other documents concerning the history of the district are to be attached, it makes no reference to these. For sites, the question 'remarks', and for districts the question 'other items of reference', provide a specific place to elaborate foreseen but unknown information.

SYSTEMATIZATION

Recording record
No question covers this topic.

Systematics
Only the district format has a selection number, a unique identification repeated on all eight sides (four sides, front and back).

Appendix

ORIGINAL QUESTION SEQUENCE
TRANSLATED (FORM JP1)

*Ledger of National Treasures
and/or Important Cultural
Properties (architecture)*
Sign and number of the certificate
of designation
Date of designation
Owner and address of owner
Location
Name and number of buildings
Structure and style, area, height

and other details that indicate
the dimension
Year or period of construction
First construction and history
Tablet, inscription, and other
such items of reference
Number of photograph
Number of drawing

ORIGINAL QUESTION SEQUENCE
TRANSLATED (FORM JP2)

Ledger of Historic Sites,
Places of Scenic Beauty and/or
Natural Monuments
Designation
Date
Alteration
Date and number in *Official*
Gazette
Custodian
Kind
Name
Location
Causes of designation
By par., item, of criteria
Explanation
Requisites for conservation
Documents:
   No. of Reports on
   Sheets of photographs
   No. of photograph ledger
   Maps attached
   Sheets of drawings
   Sheets of engraved prints
Items concerning designated area:
   Total area of lands
   Total number of lots
   Land in government possession
   Number of lots
   Acreage
   Land in private possession
   Number of lots
   Acreage
   District, city ward
   Town, village
   Major section
   Minor section
   Lot number
   Land category
   Acreage
   Name and address of owner and possessor
   Remarks

ORIGINAL QUESTION SEQUENCE
TRANSLATED (FORM JP3)

Ledger of Important Preservation
Districts for Groups of Historic
Buildings
Number of selection
Name
Number of announcement in the
   Official Gazette
   Date of selection
   Location
   Area
   Range
Name
Number of announcement in the
   Official Gazette
   Date of alteration
   Location
   Area
   Range
Requisites for conservation
Criteria for selection
Announcement in the *Official*
Gazette
Explanation for selection
Applied for selection by
municipality:
   Name
   Date of determination
   Number of announcement in the
   Official Gazette
   Location
   Area
   Date of alteration
   City planning area and district
   within or without
   Alteration dates
Regulation for preservation
   Name
   Date of establishment
   Number of announcement
   Date of enforcement
   Date of alteration
   Number of announcement
Related regulations and rules
   Name
   Date of announcement
   Number of announcement
Preservation plan
   Name
   Date of announcement
   Number of announcement
   Outline
   Other items of reference
   Population
   Number of households
   Number of houses
   Number of buildings
   Contents of measures taken
   by municipality.

Mexico (MX)

Catalogación Sistema Culhuacán

Based on information supplied by
Carlos Chanfon-Olmos, former Director

Discussion

OBJECTIVES AND STATISTICS

The Catalogación Sistema Culhuacán is operated by the Dirección de Monumentos Históricos, a department of the Instituto Nacional de Antropología e Historia. The system was designed: (a) to provide basic information on location and general characteristics of buildings with cultural value for all Mexico that would be available for immediate use by the general public, researchers and the personnel of the Dirección de Monumentos Históricos; (b) to provide concise, objective up-to-date information as a basis for planning more in-depth catalogues; (c) to ensure both the ready availability of such data and the on-going inclusion of new entries; and (d) to make the greatest possible use of the advantages of computerization within the limits of professional, technical and financial resources.

The Catalogación Sistema Culhuacán is named after the ex-Augustinian convent in which it was originally housed. The system was designed to be 'an inventory, an ordered set of basic data on the location and general characteristics of all monuments within a specific geographic area and to be neither a product of, nor subject to, individual judgement, but, rather, objective'. In view of the limited financing, a data-collection method was developed that could make use of all available human resources, from ordinary citizens to specialized researchers.

Systematic recording began in March 1971 and the first stage of work was completed in 1973 with 13,000 entries. The computer budget for this period was 122,000 pesos ($9,760) at a cost-per-building entry of 9.38 pesos ($0.75).

STAFF

The system operates with seven full-time staff; two of these are architects with Master's degrees in architecture, four have completed secondary school, one is a secretary-typist. More than twenty specialists in history, archaeology, art history, anthropology, photogrammetry, and photo interpretation have assisted in the project. Several official institutions collaborated as well.

The largest portion of the work-force, however, was made up of volunteers. Some 4,000 parish priests and 3,500 municipal delegates completed survey forms. These were checked by office staff and coded for computerization.

CRITERIA

The Catalogación Sistema Culhuacán is selective, based on the volunteer recorders' knowledge of buildings possessing some historical value and dating fom 1521 to 1900. This time-limit is required by the federal historic buildings law; all entries are protected by that law.

METHOD

During the design of the system it was decided to obtain data from survey forms sent to local civil and religious authorities. This idea was proposed to all state governors, archbishops, bishops and prelates. These authorities sent preliminary letters to mayors and parish priests within their jurisdiction informing them of the effort and requesting them to comply with the system directives.

The Catalogación Sistema Culhuacán then, at different times, sent to the priests and mayors different forms requesting the same basic information. Thus, the data received from the two volunteer groups could be cross-checked by office staff before coding. More than 80 per cent of those who received forms completed and returned them.

The volunteer recording system was found to be ideal for use with church and civil authorities in rural areas or medium-sized communities, although it did not work in large towns. The current stage of the programme is the development of an inventory of urban buildings. This information will also be coded and fed into the data bank.

Aerial photographs

To compensate for any oversight by the volunteers and in order to complete the inventory by including all possibilities, aerial photographs were to be studied. Training in photo interpretation was begun but although the initial training course was successful, budget limitations prevented continuation.

Photographs and plans

Volunteers were requested to send in exterior and interior photographs as well as plans if possible. More than 3,000 photographs and 600 plans were submitted

The forms

Information is recorded in Spanish. While one form was sent to parish priests and another to municipal delegates, both ask approximately the same questions but in a different sequence. One form for religious architecture and another for monuments and places of natural beauty will be analysed below. Although no lexicon or manual exists, clarification of the computerized questions is given in 'Sistematización de datos' in *Arquitectura religiosa* (INAH, 1972) and *Monumentos y lugares de belleza natural* (INAH, 1973), both of which are published computer indices.

The religious architecture form is a grid of eight lines with each line modified by nine unnumbered questions. This describes the major church and up to seven other religious structures within each parish. One of the nine questions, *'forma de atrio'*, is a schematic illustration. The monuments form is used for all building types as well as places of natural beauty. This is a grid of ten lines for ten possible entries. Each line is modified by five unnumbered questions.

COMPUTERIZATION

Data processing is done by DETENAL, Dirección de Estudios del Territorio Nacional, using an IBM system. Originally the inventory was coded for BULL used by the Museo de Antropología.

The religious architecture and monuments/places data is kept in separate files. Entry length is eighty spaces; one line per entry. Entry is by free text, keyword and numeric codes. Free text is used for town or city, address, and name of monument or church. Monastic order is by keyword. Alpha-numeric codes are used for all other questions. Print-out is the standard 132-space line.

USERS AND PRODUCTS

An important intangible result of the inventory method is the sensitizing of 7,500 volunteers to the architecture of their immediate vicinities as well as to the importance of the project.

Other products of the system include the collected photographs and plans submitted by volunteers and the various print-out indices produced from the collected information. While not designed for direct publication, data have been used in the preparation of fundamental architectural studies. Some computer listings have been published for handy reference such as the *Monumentos y lugares de belleza natural* and *Arquitectura religiosa de los siglos XVI a XIX*.

Computerized information is available to the general public and scholarly researchers at the data bank of the Dirección de Estudios del Territorio Nacional (DETENAL) and has been used for preparation of maps and charts of cultural and tourism resources.

Summary/Evaluation

The Catalogación Sistema Culhuacán has many strong points. It has made extraordinary use of 7,500 volunteers for the economical collection of basic data. Print-out is available for use by the general public as well as researchers. One eighty-space line per entry is economical for storage and can be easily updated. Coded information is standardized and easy to read and compare.

The three-digit date is terse. Local fiesta dates not only provide historical commentary but signal possible conservation problems caused by unauthorized fiesta-related alterations The date of the earliest document in the parish archives aids researchers as does the office file number for monuments. Questions on plan, roof and retables describe religious structures.

However, there are problems with the system. Using mayors and priests as volunteers for data collection proved unsuccessful in larger urban areas. Selection criteria is subjective based on a local knowledge of buildings having some historical value as viewed by ordinary citizens. Office staff had to cross-check as well as code volunteer forms before computerization.

Forms are not titled, and questions are generally unnumbered. Spaces for hand-written answers are small. Few instructions appear on the forms and no lexicon is available. On the print-out neither the parish nor municipality is decoded. Monument type is identified in the '*sistematización de datos*' but numerically coded in all print-out thus requiring a constant referral to ascertain, for example, that 06 stands for '*iglesia con otra función*'.

Question analysis

An analysis of the kinds of information required for the religious architecture form and another for monuments and places follows. Analysis is by category and not by the question sequence on the forms. For a question-by-question comparison of these Mexican questions with the other systems, see Part Three.

IDENTIFICATION/LOCATION

Both forms name the town (*población*). Neither asks for the state, but the information is computerized. Municipality is combined with town on the religious form but not computerized; municipality is not asked for on the monuments form but is computerized using codes established separately by the Dirección Général de Estadística.

On the religious form the parish is not stated, but it is computerized in numeric code with the major parish church marked 'A' and other religious structures in the same parish marked 'B—Z'. The name of each church (*advocación*) is given and the religious order (*orden monástica original*).

The monuments form preprints the various types of monuments or place; the correct answer is checked. Addresses are given only on this form as street and number of suburb/neighbourhood, or distance in kilometres from town.

SIGNIFICANCE/DESIGNATION

No question covers this category but all entries are protected by federal law.

DATE/HISTORY

Both forms ask for the date, which is computerized in arabic numerals by century third. For example, the last third of the sixteenth century is coded '16 3'.

For religious architecture, the day and month of up to three local fiestas are recorded. The religious order that constructed the church is identified. Additional information regarding legends or traditions is collected, but not computerized.

DESCRIPTION

The religious form provides a physical descrip-tion of the entry. Separate questions describe roof shape and number of towers. Atriums and crossings are noted. Retables are counted.

CONSERVATION/RESTORATION/PRESERVATION

No questions on either form specifically discuss this category, although two questions on the Religious Architecture form are relevant. If the church is in ruins, this is noted under 'religious order'. Dates of local fiestas provide maintenance information since 'fiestas are reputed to be the most common pretext for unauthorized altera-tions'.

DOCUMENTATION/REFERENCE

The religious architecture form cites the date of the oldest document in the parish archives. For monuments the office file number is compu-terized but not asked for on the form. Volunteers were requested to send exterior and interior photographs and plans if possible. The existence of this information is not computerized.

SYSTEMATIZATION

No questions cover this category.

Appendix
ORIGINAL QUESTION SEQUENCE
AND TRANSLATION (FORM MX1)

Cuestionario No. 1	*Questionnaire 1*
1. ¿Qué monumentos religiosos construidos en el periodo 1521 a 1900 existen en su parroquia? Llenado este cuadro, díganos los mayores detalles de cada monumento	Religious architecture
Nombre de la población y del municipio	Town Municipality
Advocación	Name of church
Fecha aproximada	Approximate date
Orden monástica original	Religious order
Forma de atrio	Atrium
Cruz atrial	Crossing
Número de torres	Number of towers
Techo de la nave principal	Roof
Retablos importantes	Number of retables
2. ¿Se conservan en buen estado los archivos parroquiales? Díganos desde qué epoca existen documentos	(Oldest document in parish archives)
3. ¿En qué fechas se acostumbra en esa parroquia celebrar ferias y fiestas tradicionales?	Dates of festivals

4. ¿Qué leyendas y tradiciones religiosas o profanas existen en la parroquia a su cargo?

Legends and traditions

5. Mandar fotografías exteriores e interiores y planos si es posible.

Photographs and plans, if possible

ORIGINAL QUESTION SEQUENCE AND TRANSLATION (FORM MX2)

Población (Localización): Nombre de la calle y número, colonia o barrio km carretera, etc. Nombre del monumento o del lugar de belleza natural, paseo, parque, jardín, etc.

(Monuments and places form) Town (Address): Street and number, suburb or neighbourhood, road milepost, etc. Name of monument or place of natural beauty, avenue, park garden, etc.

Año o siglo aproximado	Approximate year or century
Casa	House
Edificio	Building
Hacienda	Estate
Iglesia en servicio	Church in use
Iglesia con otra función	Church with other function
Fuerte	Fort
Monumento conmemorativo	Commemorative monument
Fuente	Spring
Acueducto	Aqueduct
Puente	Bridge
Faro	Lighthouse
Playa	Beach
Lago	Lake
Cascada	Waterfall
Peñasco	Rocks
Bosque	Woods
Gruta	Grotto
Otros	Other

Morocco (MA)

Inventaire National du Patrimoine Culturel

Based on information supplied by
Abdelhaid El Badmoussi, Chef du Service,
Documentation Bibliographique, Icono-
graphique et Sonore

Discussion

OBJECTIVES AND STATISTICS

The Inventaire National du Patrimoine Culturel is a division of the Ministère d'Etat Chargé des Affaires Culturelles. Its principal task is to prepare an exhaustive list of everything of historic, scientific, ethnographic and artistic value for the nation. The Inventaire is carried out by type of cultural property as well as by geographical region.

Immovable cultural property, monuments and sites, are surveyed to integrate them into national policies of preservation and development. Based on the findings of the inventory some entries are proposed for further protection, restoration and development.

Work on the methodology began in October 1974 with the help of a Unesco expert. The Inventory Division was established by Decree 275.443, Chaabane 1395/26 August 1975. There is no autonomous budget.

It is difficult to foresee either the date of completion or the final number of entries. As at 31 December 1980, close to 600 monuments and sites were classified. Classification implies obligatory legal protection measures.

STAFF

The system has a staff of twelve with specialities in cultural anthropology and ethnology (1), information science (4), sociology (1), law (1), and photography/reprography (5).

CRITERIA

The section of the Inventaire dealing with monuments and sites includes individual build-ings and structures, ensembles and groups, villages, natural features, national parks, architectural and urban elements, and archaeological sites. The archaeological sites are inventoried in collaboration with the Archaeological Service of the same ministry.

The Inventaire is selective, based on historical, archaeological and architectural criteria. Priority is given to the most remarkable examples. The actual state of conservation influences the choice; the poorer the condition of the structure the less likely it is to be included. For natural sites, aesthetic, artistic and legendary aspects are considered.

METHOD

Research is done by office staff based on published sources. Reports are prepared and subsequently researchers make site visits using the prepared reports as reference. More than ninety such analytic studies have been made.

At the moment of research, whether it be in the office or at the site, a working form is completed. After verification by two specialized staff members, these data are typed in their final version on the appropriate permanent site or monument forms.

The forms

Three basic forms are used by the Inventaire for immovable cultural property. The Liste Générale des Monuments et Sites is a computerized format which asks approximately fourteen questions. Both the site and monument forms are manual. No handbook or lexicon exists for the system. All questions are in French and unnumbered.

The site form, which asks approximately thirty questions, is used to record situations that include landscapes considered for picturesque qualities, ensembles (collection of objects having common attributes) and groups (villages, urban quarters, etc.). The monument form is for an individual object such as a structure, building or natural feature which may also be part of a larger site.

All entries are classified by the Nomenclature Typologique which is a listing of sixty-five particular types of sites and monuments. Approximately twenty of these types are Arabic terms such as *kasba, ksar, medina* and *marabout*.

COMPUTERIZATION

Computerization of the Inventaire National du Patrimoine is presently under development using MINISIS. The Liste Générale form is designed for computerization. Eight lines of seventy-three spaces each provide the information which is entered in free text, keywords and codes.

Free text is used for the name of the entry, circle, town, commune or *douar*. Keywords include the type of legal status, protection decision, Lambert cartographic zone and map sheet, Hegira month, and remarks. Other dates, type-order number, province, line number, Lambert co-ordinates and decision number are coded alpha-numerically.

Every line repeats the unique type-order number for each entry and the province code. Each line also has a 'c.c.' number which identifies the line and, thus, the information stored on the line. For lines that are repeated, the count of the line is also given. For example, three different sets of information for Line 6 can be coded for each entry by assigning the 'c.c.' numbers 6/1, 6/2, 6/3. Each covers a separate protection decision, Christian (A.D.) and Islamic (Hegira) dates, decision number and remark.

USERS AND PRODUCTS

All Inventaire National resources are used by the staff of the Ministry of Cultural Affairs as well as researchers, historians, architects, archaeologists, and university students. Several features of the Inventaire allow retrospective research of the monuments and sites: the photo file (*photothèque*), the microfiche file (*microthèque*) containing 7,000 documents and the bibliographic index containing 5,000 references to Moroccan cultural heritage. Three computer-generated volumes of this index have been published under the title, *Fichier-index bibliographique du patrimoine culturel*, by the Ministère d'État Chargé des Affaires Culturelles. It covers works published in Morocco or abroad indexed by keyword, author and main citation.

Primary products of the sites and monuments inventory are the completed individual forms with their attached plans, drawings, and photographs as well as the computerized format of the Liste Générale which provides basic location, identification and legal status information for each entry.

In addition more than ninety analytic studies have been prepared by the staff covering such diverse topics as *kasbas* and *art rupestre* (rock art). Special efforts have been made to integrate both of these important cultural resources into national protection and development policies. The rock-art study was published in 1977 under the title, *Catalogue des sites rupestres du Sud-Marocain*, by the Ministère d'Etat Chargé des Affaires Culturelles.

Summary/Evaluation

The Moroccan Inventaire National du Patrimoine Culturel is an ambitious project to record all the cultural properties of the nation. The sites and monuments inventory utilizes manual forms to collect information first from published sources and subsequently from site visits. The distinctive Nomenclature Typologique incorporates many particularly Arabic terms. Expressing dates by the Muslim system, as well as the Christian, reflects the Islamic culture of the country. All collected data are objective and factual, but the scope is selective. Only the most remarkable examples of sites and monuments in better states of conservation are listed. Emphasis is placed on the protection of the entries by legal decrees and the necessary conservation work. Some boxed answers and pre-printed controlled responses are an aid to the completion of forms.

Unfortunately, no manual or handbook exists for the system. Computerization is still under development. Questions are unnumbered. Long statements and paragraphs of text preclude easy eventual total computerization. The cross-references between type-order numbers for monuments within sites, although necessary, is confusing. The Nomenclature Typologique is not hierarchical. For example, '06 cascade', 08 *cours d'eau*', and '13 *forêt*' are all natural features but are neither grouped together under one heading nor numbered in sequence. To search for all natural features within such a list each individual type needs to be searched separately, i.e. 06, 08, 13, etc.

Question analysis

An analysis of the kinds of information asked on the List, Site and Monument forms follows. Most questions are answered in brief text statements. Other than the type-order number there are few coded questions. Analysis here is by category and not by the sequence of questions on the forms. For a question-by-question comparison of these Moroccan questions contrasted with the other systems, see Part Three.

IDENTIFICATION/LOCATION

Province, circle, commune, town and place are all established. The monument form combines commune and town; on the list, place or quarter is excluded. All forms require geographic coordinates, citing the Lambert sheet number and zones. The monument form, in addition includes cadastre references. On all forms the actual name of the site or monument is given as well as the type-order number which codes the type (*ksar, cascade,* etc.) from the Nomenclature Typologique and the actual numeric sequence within that typology. The monument form also states present use, which is not the typology but what it is used for, such as habitat. The evolution of use, plus proposed and possible uses, are all given in text statements. Both the site and monument forms ask for the owner or the responsible administration.

SIGNIFICANCE/DESIGNATION

No form asks for significance but all three state the legal status including the actual decree, date and number. Three separate legal decisions with dates and numbers can be computerized on the List. Christian (A.D.) and Islamic (Hegira) dates are both cited on this form. On the site and monuments forms the need for protection can be expressed as well.

DATE/HISTORY

Only the List asks for the precise date of the structure which may be plus or minus and A.D. or Hegira for archaeological, Christian and Islamic precision. The monument form asks for the construction period. Both the site and monument forms request history and popular traditions. No reference is made to builder or architect.

DESCRIPTION

Both the site and monument forms provide short general paragraphs of description. The monument form further adds setting and contents (*cadre et contenu*), particular characteristics, materials, and a discussion of any movable works of art contained within.

CONSERVATION/RESTORATION/PRESERVATION

Both the monument and site forms ask for the present state of the entry which, on the monument form, is combined with observations. The site form also asks for possible dangers as well as future development perspectives. For monuments, the state of conservation is checked off in boxes pre-printed with 'satisfactory', 'mediocre' and 'bad' as choices. The state of the total work, its parts, roof, ceiling/terrace and interior are all indicated, as well as humidity level and condensation. The degree of needed conservation is similarly pre-printed to be checked. Two additional questions in text, give technical data on existing or proposed restoration.

DOCUMENTATION/REFERENCE

Basic bibliography is cited on both the site and monument forms. They also cite other documentary sources including studies and reports, plans and maps, photographs, slides, films and others archives. On the monuments form these categories are checked off in a pre-printed box and the full identification completed. For the site form graphic, photographic and cartographic documentation is attached on the reverse. For monuments, graphic and photographic documentation is attached at the bottom of the form. For monuments one question, 'observations', records the 'unknown whatevers'.

SYSTEMATIZATION

Recording record

Both the monument and site forms name the drafter, checker and reviser of the form and give the date. This is asked for on front and back of the monument form. Both forms also name the site inspector, date of inspection and inspection file number.

Systematics

All three forms cite the unique six-digit type-order number for each entry. The first two digits code the appropriate Nomenclature Typologique (*ksar, cascade,* etc.) and the next four digits provide the actual numeric sequence within that typology. Sites and Monuments use the same typology list but cross-reference their different typology numbers.

For example, the site type-order number may be 22.0001. This represents Typology 22, *ksar* (fortified southern village), and 0001 for the first such entry in the Inventaire. Part of this site is Monument 20.0046 which is Type 20, *tighremt* (citadel), and 0046 for the forty-sixth example within the entire system. The site monument cross-reference then is Site 22.0001, cf. Monument 20.0046.

Appendix

Liste Générale des Monuments et Sites	*General List of Monuments and Sites*
Nom du monument ou du site	Name of monument/site
Date	Date
Type-no. d'ordre	Type-order number
C.C.	Computer line number
Province	Province
Cercle	Circle
Ville	Town
Type-no. d'ordre	Type-order number
C.C.	Computer line number
Province	Province
Commune urbaine ou rurale (*douar*)	Urban commune or rural *douar*
Type-no. d'ordre	Type-order number
C.C.	Computer line number
Province	Province
Décision de protection	Protection decision
Date (agr. J.-C.)	Date (A.D.)
Date (hégire)	Date (Hegira)
Numéro	Number
Remarque	Remark
Type-no. d'ordre	Type-order number
C.C.	Computer line number
Province	Province
Localisation exacte	Exact co-ordinates
Type-no. d'ordre	Type-order number
C.C.	Computer line number
Province	Province
Statut foncier actuel et/ou en voie d'adoption	Legal Status present or underway
Type-no. d'ordre	Type-order number
C.C.	Computer line number
Province	Province
Décision de protection	Protection decision
Date (apr. J.-C.)	Date (A.D.)
Date (Hegira)	Date (Hegira)
Numéro	Number
Remarque	Remark
Type-no. d'ordre	Type-order number
C.C.	Computer line number
Province	Province

Site	*Site form*
No.	Type-order number
Cf. Monument No.	Cf. number
Province	Province
Cercle	Circle
Commune	Commune
Lieu-dit	Place
Situation exacte et limites de zones	Exact location and limits of zones
Dénomination	Name
Propriétaire; administration responsable	Owner; responsible office
Description	Description
Histoire et traditions populaires	History and popular traditions
État actuel	Present state
Dangers éventuels	Eventual dangers
Perspectives de développement	Development perspectives
Protection existante	Present protection
Degré de protection	Degree of protection
Protection prévue	Future protection
Bibliographie de base	Basic bibliography
Visité par	Visited by
Date	Date
No. du dossier	File number
Autres sources documentaires—origine	Other documentary sources
Études et rapports	Studies and reports
Plans et cartes	Plans and maps
Photographies	Photographs
Diapositives	Slides
Films	Films
Autres archives	Other archives
Observations	Observations
Rédigée par: le (date)	Drafted by and date
Contrôlée par: le (date)	Checked by and date
Révisée par: le (date)	Revised by and date

Monument	*Monument form*
No.	Type-order number
Cf. Site no.	Cf. Site number
Province, chef-lieu	Province, main place
Cercle	Circle
Ville, commune	Town, commune
Quarter, lieu-dit	Quarter, place
Situation exacte	Exact location
Cadastre	Cadastre
Dénomination	Name
Propriétaire; administration responsable	Owner; responsible office
Cadre et contenu	Setting and contents
Époque de construction	Construction period
Utilisation actuelle	Present use
Description	Description
Œuvres d'art mobilières	Movable works of art
État actuel, observations	Present state, observations
État de conservation	State of conservation
Degré de protection à appliquer	Degree of (conservation) needed
Protection légale	Legal protection
Nature de la décision	Type of decision
Rédigée par: le (date)	Drafted by and date
Contrôlée par: le (date)	Checked by and date
Révisée par: le (date)	Revised by and date

Données typologiques
Histoire et traditions populaires
Caractéristiques particulières
Données chronologiques
Évolution subie
Utilisation proposée
Utilisation possible
Données techniques
Matériaux
Opérations de restauration (en cours ou à l'étude)
Perspectives de restauration
Visité par: le (date)

Typological data
History and popular traditions
Particular characteristics

Chronological data
Evolution
Proposed use
Possible use
Technical data
Materials
Restoration work (underway or studied)

Restoration perspectives

Visited by and date

No. du dossier
Bibliographie de base
Observations, dangers éventuels
Rédigée par: le (date)
Contrôlée par: le (date)
Révisée par: le (date)
Autres sources documentaires—origine
Etudes et rapports
Cartes
Plans
Photographies
Diapositives
Films
Autres archives

File number
Basic bibliography
Observations, eventual dangers
Drafted by and date
Checked by and date
Revised by and date
Other documentary sources
Studies and reports
Maps
Plans
Photographs
Slides
Films
Other archives

New York City (NYC)

Urban Cultural Resources Survey (UCRS)

Written by
Meredith H. Sykes, former Director of Survey.

Discussion

OBJECTIVES AND STATISTICS

The Urban Cultural Resources Survey is a programme of the New York City Landmarks Preservation Commission. Based on the Canadian Inventory of Historic Building, this survey was designed to furnish detailed, computerized information on all extant building exteriors and important urban design features of the city. The survey helps the Landmarks Preservation Commission, the nation's largest municipal preservation agency, establish priorities for legal designation.

Designation decisions, based upon an analysis of the total fabric of the city's structural environment, could be accomplished only with a comprehensive computerized survey. All buildings and features are considered not as isolated entities but in terms of the other existing examples which may be comparable in style, period or level of significance. The UCRS records non-designated entries as well as landmarks and historic districts designated at the local and federal levels.

Systematic site recording began in June 1979. As at 31 December 1980, there were 50,000 entries. The estimated number of entries upon completion of the comprehensive survey will be 850,000 to 1 million. The final date of completion cannot be foreseen. The original budget, much of which was provided by one-time grants and special funds, was $350,000.

STAFF

A full-time professional survey staff of fifteen permanent and contract positions includes thirteen recorders who hold graduate degrees in art history, architectural history, or preservation, and two professional photographers.

In addition, at any one period, approximately 100 volunteers provide assistance. Volunteers may be secondary-school or college students or local residents. Besides establishing community support for the survey, the volunteers themselves gain a heightened appreciation of the architectural assets of their own neighbourhoods. There is a three-session training programme for volunteers.

CRITERIA

The UCRS is comprehensive. All existing building exteriors and important urban design features of the five boroughs of the city are to be recorded. There is no cut-off date or time frame, although buildings less than thirty years old cannot be considered for designation as city landmarks. Information on earlier buildings known only by research can be accommodated within the system, though these are generally not recorded. An urban archaeology component is under development.

Areas to be recorded are selected by the survey director in consultation with the executive staff of the commission. Recorders are always assigned a particular area in which they record and photograph every immovable feature.

METHOD

The UCRS is open-ended. New question-and-answer choices can be added. All seventy-six questions and their precoded answer choices are listed in the codes. In addition, a continuous alphabetical list of all precoded answers (more than 1,000 terms) has been prepared. 'Notes' provide instructions for completing the field form as well as definitions of questions.

Hierarchical codes

The codes for uses and materials are hierarchically structured. Use is divided into twenty-eight generic categories which modify 301 particular possibilities. The ultimate possibility in each category is always 99, or 'other'. When additional particular uses are discovered they may be assigned the next highest number in the generic category and added to the open-ended list.

In addition to basic-use categories for buildings (residential, religious, etc.) several urban feature categories include spatial, view and vista, landscaping, as well as civic art, street furniture, and roadway elements.

The materials list is also hierarchical. Nine generic categories divide eighty-eight particular kinds. From both materials and uses lists it is possible to code and search either a specific or the generic: for example, specific, glazed terracotta, —generic, all ceramic materials; specific, a water vista—generic, all views and vistas.

The geocode

The main identity number of all entries and the nucleus of the system is the geocode. Assigned only by staff, thirteen digits code four elements: the city borough, block, lot and parcel which comprise the legal reference for each New York City building. The parcel is coded when two or more entries occupy the same lot. Non-buildings such as lamp-posts, sidewalks, etc., are coded as tangent to the lot. Earlier buildings no longer extant but known from historical research, as well as urban archaeology features found below grade, can all be coded using the parcel number. Thus, with the geocode it is possible to provide information detailing any block and lot in New York City as it is at the time of recording as well as what is tangent to that lot and how the lot appeared in the past both above and below the surface.

Photography

Every entry in the UCRS is photographed on 35 mm black-and-white film. Volunteer recorders are furnished with film if they have an appropriate camera. All film rolls are numbered sequentially and the frames for each entry are noted. Photo information is computerized. The first photograph taken on the roll is an identification picture of the roll number and the photographer's name.

Film is processed in the office and two sets of contact prints produced. One is stored with the negatives and a list of addresses of buildings and features pictured on that roll. The other is cut and the individual pictures are attached to photo cards for the office files. Each office photo card also repeats basic identification and location information.

The field form

The UCRS field form is divided into three vertical columns with each horizontal line having space for a written answer to a question, blank spaces to code it, and associated computer fields to guide key punchers. During street recording all answers are generally written first in text and then transcribed into numeric codes and entered in the second column. Numbers and titles of the first forty-five questions are printed on the form. Each of these questions is generally answered for every entry. The second part of the form, called 'random questions', deals principally with a building's physical description. Here a recorder can enter up to twenty answers in any sequence from a pre-coded list of thirty questions (Nos. 46–76 in the codes). These usually describe a building's elements or parts such as windows, roof shape, etc. In addition, each answer can be modified by its own style, material and location.

COMPUTERIZATION

Record length is fixed at 560 spaces or 7 lines. Each line repeats the geocode in Spaces 1–13; Space 80 provides the line number. Entry is in numeric code and all data are stored as numerics. Print-out is available as either numerics or keywords. The software is CMS; all programs are written in PL/1. Mark IV is used for report generating.

Data entry (key punching on to magnetic tape) is contracted out; computer processing is provided by the Computer Service Center of the City of New York. Two CRT terminals with telephone hook-ups are used to link the survey office with the main data base. On-line information is in numerics.

Computerized indices can be in numerics or in keywords. Data retrieval is fast and flexible. Searches or sorts can be run on any question(s), answer(s), or combination(s). Listings may be printed in any sequence by any question(s), or answer(s), or combination(s).

All data may be given for each selection or only some. Thus it is possible to search for all Manhattan buildings dating from pre-1850 that are of Georgian style and currently used for residential purposes. Data may be requested as listed alphabetically by street name with ascending numeric addresses and descending dates, or otherwise.

USERS AND PRODUCTS

The primary users of the UCRS are the staff of the Landmarks Preservation Commission. The UCRS provides a systematic comparative analysis of the total urban fabric in order that priorities for landmark designation can be established throughout the city. Additional print-out data and photographs are provided to other municipal, state and federal agencies. Information is available to scholars and researchers. Film-makers have used the data to find film locations.

Products of the system are the black-and-white photographs of all entries and the computerized recording form and indices. Print-out is provided in either numerics or easily understood keywords. Film roll and negatives are computerized so that photographs illustrating the recorded data can be provided easily. Photographs to illustrate the entire UCRS code of more than 1,000 terms can be searched automatically in question-and-answer sequence and listed by film roll and frame plus address.

Summary/Evaluation

The UCRS was designed to furnish detailed computerized information to enable the Landmarks Preservation Commission to set priorities for designation based on an analysis of the total fabric of New York City. Since mid-1979 it has been in operation as a computerized method to record all extant building exteriors and important design features. Criteria for buildings are comprehensive and all-inclusive. There is no time-frame or cut-off date.

The UCRS can be used by both volunteers and professional staff. The methodology is explained in notes, while codes lists all questions and precoded answers. Answers are written in text on the field form and then coded numerically. At the text level the system can be used manually. With the geocode it is possible to provide information describing any block and lot as it was at the time of recording and what was tangent to it, as well as what past structures once existed on that lot and what urban archaeological remains are known to lie below. The unique 'random questions' format allows multiple answers combining choice, style, material and location.

All entries are photographed with standard 35 mm black-and-white film and the photographic record is computerized. Precoded answers make data easy to compare. Computerized print-out indices are possible in any combination of questions and answers. The system is open-ended; both questions and answers can be expanded.

However, there are problems. The task is immense and the means are limited. There is no standardized recording record; recorder and date are not recorded. Not enough possibilities are provided for historical dates and architects' names. Significance is a subjective question based on the recorder's evaluation of aesthetic importance. Coding all building, architects and community names into numerics is tedious; free text

might be used, yet this would greatly increase the entry length.

Economic data storage in numerics is necessary to handle the potential 1 million entries, but this precluded immediate on-line access by keyword. Thus the present on-line system cannot be interrogated by the general public. Updating is difficult due to the length of each entry (seven lines) and permanent data storage on magnetic tape.

Question analysis

An analysis of the kinds of information asked for on the UCRS field form follows. Every question is computerized. All random questions are multiple choice and can be answered as often as needed. Analysis is by category and not by the question sequence on the form. For a question-by-question comparison of these New York City questions contrasted with the other systems see Part Three.

IDENTIFICATION/LOCATION

For location the borough, block, lot, parcel are combined into the geocode. In addition the community name, street, number(s) on the street and any additional street and number are given. A standard street master list precoded for use by all city departments is used for this. If the entry faces two streets, the additional street address is noted. Community names are used to identify neighbourhoods and historic districts. These are written in text and assigned a number from the office code book.

The present name, original name and complex name are all asked. The complex name modifies a group of structures each of which may also be individually named. Names are written in text and assigned a number from the office code book.

Two present uses and two original uses are possible. Either specific use (religious–rectory) or only generic use (religious) may be coded. Original use is gleaned from research. Abandoned/ruin and vacant/uninhabited are generic categories of use.

SIGNIFICANCE/DESIGNATION

One question, significance, combines levels of aesthetic importance with levels of local or federal designation. Only non-designated entries are judged for significance. All non-designated entries graded as typical or outstanding examples of a given style are further researched to determine factual dates and architects. Levels of official designation include New York City landmarks (exterior, interior, scenic, and historic districts) and federal landmarks (National Historic Landmark or National Register).

DATE/HISTORY

Original date and date of change are cited. Dates are coded in three digits, 1865 becomes 865. If the date is not known from research it is marked 'estimated'. Demolition after recording is coded as date-of-change and the entry is updated.

Socio-historic significance considers non-aesthetic importance such as a specific battle site, birthplace, etc. This is written in text and assigned a numeric code from the office code book.

Primary architect and/or firm and secondary architect and/or firm are identified. Such information is gleaned from research. Each name is written in text and assigned a numeric code from the office code book.

DESCRIPTION

Property features such as outbuildings and fences are listed in a random question. The depth and width, both of the building and plot, are given in feet. The number of bays and storeys, existence of an attic and/or visible basement, massing, architectural and elevational compositions and plan types are described. When structures on the same street are either identical or mirror images this is noted as well as the address of their peers. Only one such structure need then be coded completely.

Up to three separate styles may describe the total entry. In addition each random-question answer can be modified by its own style.

Many building elements can be coded in separate random questions: chimneys; dormers; entrance location; door—opening, trim, type, panels; porch; window—opening, trim, panes; architectural sculpture and art; decorative motifs; modifiers; building features; and interior items of interest. The construction technique is given and the materials of the façade, trim and of any random question answered. Applied surface coatings such as paint or gilt can be noted.

CONSERVATION/RESTORATION/PRESERVATION

No questions discuss conservation as such. Several questions express the actual condition of the entry. Two modifiers, 'original or unaltered' and 'vandalized or ruinous' can describe the present state of any random-question answer. Alterations or additions to a storey can also be noted.

DOCUMENTATION/REFERENCE

Research Resources lists other surveys known to include the building such the HABS (Historic American Building Survey).The UCRS film-roll number and picture numbers are given, as well as any additional rolls and pictures.

SYSTEMATIZATION

Recording record

Although no recording record is made of the street survey, the year of inspection by staff, concerning demolition permits, is coded.

Systematics

Each entry is assigned a unique geocode of coded borough, block, lot and parcel information which precedes, in thirteen digits, every record or line of the seven-line entry. Every record or line is identified with a pre-printed record number. Numbers of computer fields are pre-printed following each answer code blank to guide the key-puncher to the correct space on the line. Completed forms are grouped in batches of 1,000 for computer punching; each batch is assigned a number.

Appendix

ORIGINAL QUESTION SEQUENCE
(FORM NYC)

1. Borough
2. Block
3. Lot
4. Part
5. Street
6. Numeric address
7. Non-numeric address
8. Also known as street
9. Also known as numeric
10. Community
11. Film-roll No.
12. Film shot, first
13. Film shot, last
14. Present use (1)
15. Present use (2)
16. Original use (1)
17. Original use (2)
18. Style (1)
19. Style (2)
20. Style (3)
21. Significance
    Batch No.
    Record No. 1
    Geocode No.
22. Present name
23. Original name
24. Complex name
25. Original date
26. If estimated
27. Date of change
28. If estimated
29. Primary architect
30. Of firm

31. Secondary architect
32. Of firm
33. Massing of structure
    Record No. 2
    Geocode No.
34. Number of units
35. Unit, mirror image
36. Same as street
37. Same as number
38. Plot width in feet
39. Plot depth in feet
40. Building width in feet
41. Building depth in feet
42. Storeys
43. Basement
44. Attic
45. Bays
    Record No. 3

Random questions
46. Façade material
47. Trim material
48. Alterations to storey
49. Entrance location
50. Door opening

51. Door trim
52. Door type
53. Panels
54. Porch
55. Window opening
56. Window trim
57. Window type
58. Window panes
59. Roof shape
60. Roof trim
61. Roof features
62. Chimneys
63. Dormer roof
64. Building features
65. Property features
66. Decorative motifs
67. Surface coating
68. Architectural composition
69. Significant interior space
70. Architectural sculpture and art
71. Modifiers
72. Research resources
73. Elevational composition
74. Construction technique
75. Plan
76. Socio-historic significance

Poland (PL)

System of Inventorying Historical Monuments

Based on information supplied by
Marek Konopka, Vice-director, Historical
Monuments Documentation Centre

Discussion

OBJECTIVES AND STATISTICS

The Polish System for Inventorying Historical Monuments is centrally organized, planned, and supervised by the Historical Monuments Documentation Centre, which is part of the Ministry of Culture and Arts. It is the centre's chief, though not single, area of activity. Several individual surveys make up the effort: (a) the Inventory of the Immovable Historical Monuments (monuments), (b) the Inventory of Historical Cities and Towns (cities); (c) the Inventory of Parks, Gardens, Avenues and Cemeteries; (d) the Archaeological Map of Poland; and (e) the Inventory of the Movable Historical Monuments.

The principal objectives of the total system are: (a) the identification of historical and cultural monuments; (b) documentation to reflect clearly the historical and artistic values of the national heritage; and (c) planned protection of this heritage based on the collected documentation.

This present documentation, based on the identification and systematic recording of all existing monuments, will allow effective protection to be planned and integrated into the economic and industrial development of Poland.

Within the system, complex links need to be created to integrate the protection of the cultural heritage with the future development of the land. Protection zones need to be delimited within the framework of economic and industrial development. In order to do this, precise localization is planned for all categories of historic monuments on maps which visually combine topographic, ecologic and historical data.

The Inventory of the Immovable Historical Monuments began in 1975; the Archaeological Map in 1978. Both are expected to be completed by the year 2000. Archaeological entries total 80,000; 115,000 architectural entries have been made. The parks and gardens survey began in 1975 and will be completed by 1985; 2,862 entries have been recorded.

STAFF

Inventory information is gathered in the regions by local teams under the direction of Voivodship offices for Research and Documentation of Historical Monuments. All data are then compiled and collected at the single central archive of the Historical Monuments Documentation Centre in Warsaw. Total staff for the entire project numbers 400 highly qualified specialists. The budget is 18–20 million zlotys per year.

CRITERIA

Collected data are classified according to different categories of monuments (architecture, historic cities and towns, archaeology, movable works, etc.). Each category is organized geographically by Voivodship and locality.

The Archaeological Map records all pre-nineteenth-century work. This map and the other non-architectural surveys are comprehensive. The system is selective only for architecture, based on the opinions of experts. The cut-off date for wooden construction is pre-1914; the time limit for other buildings is generally 1939 and, rarely, 1950. Buildings destroyed and demolished since the Second World War are excluded from documentation.

METHOD

There are two phases for all recording in the Polish system. The first phase is to gather basic

83

data; the second is to complete the appropriate inventory forms as well as compiling documentation such as photographs, plans and sketches.

The scope of the five separate inventories will be briefly noted. For the purpose of this manual those two will be studied in depth which deal with architecture and town planning: the Inventory of the Immovable Historical Monuments (called Monuments here) and the Inventory of Historic Cities and Towns (Cities).

Except for the Archaeological Map all methods are described in English in *A System of Inventorying Historical Monuments in Poland,* published by the Historical Monuments Documentation Centre, in 1977. Copies of the forms, translated questions and definitions of terms are included.

The Archaeological Map of Poland was begun in 1978 to record all pre-nineteenth-century archaeology. It divides the country into standard 37.5 km² units on a base map of 1:25,000, locates each site, and integrates all documentation with graphic symbols. Information is collected on two forms. The standard inventory sheet, Karta Ewidencji Stanowiska Archaeologicznego, asks ten specific questions and provides some pre-printed answers to be checked off. A punched card (not a computer card) records the information for each archaeological site with graphic symbols as well as text. The appropriate pre-printed descriptive symbols are crossed out. For example: a balloon signifies aerial photography; a book, reference sources; and an ear, hearsay or unconfirmed data.

The Inventory of Parks, Gardens, Avenues and Cemeteries was begun in 1975 and is carried out under the supervision of the Board of Museums and Historical Monuments Protection, Ministry of Culture and Arts. This covers pre-1939 subjects. Its objectives are: (a) to determine which parks, gardens, avenues and cemeteries are to be protected in part or in whole; (b) to determine which sepulchral objects should be separately inventoried and protected; and (c) to determine the range of indispensable or desirable conservation/restoration.

The Inventory of the Movable Historical Monuments, although generally outside the scope of this manual, will be mentioned briefly. Begun in 1962, 200,000 movable monuments were recorded by 1981. Included are movable works of art or artistic crafts as well as small-sized architectural objects such as tombs, wayside shrines and crosses. Major decorative architectural elements (doorways, architraves, etc.) wall paintings, stained glass and epitaphs which may be parts of a building are, nevertheless, recorded in this format. Objects stored in museums are not included since museums keep their own documentation.

Architectural and town-planning surveys

The Inventory of Historical Cities and Towns covers all localities that are or at any time in the past were endowed with urban statutes. By 1977 some 1,400 historical cities and towns were included. A file for each locality contains such materials as a concise historical account of urban development, present-day and historical maps, photographs of town-planning features and layout. The cover sheet of each file in the Cities Inventory asks thirteen unnumbered questions which will be analysed below.

The Monuments Inventory covers architecture and buildings of all types and periods from the Middle Ages up to 1939 and, in rare instances, 1950. Two forms are used which will be analysed below. Across the top of both, alphabetic-colour codes give information to facilitate manual filing.

An address form is completed for each item exhibiting some historical features and values as well as those 'deserving to be subjected to a conservator's care'. No photograph is attached. It asks thirteen unnumbered questions.

An inventory sheet for the Monuments Inventory asks twenty-seven numbered questions on four sides and constitutes a more complete documentation record. Photographs and plans are attached on the first side. Two copies are made; one for the Historical Monuments Documentation Centre, one for the conservator of the area.

COMPUTERIZATION

The entire Polish inventory system is to be computerized. The Inventory of the Movable Historical Monuments is being converted first; keyword thesauri of terms are being compiled. Up to thirty keyword descriptors will be retrieved for each entry; additional descriptors will indicate where documentation is stored. The programming language is SEZAR for ODRA 1305 computers.

PRODUCTS AND USERS

The Historical Monuments Documentation Centre has created one central archive to compile and collect information from many disciplines according to the category of monument inventoried. This documentation is used by regional and central government offices, staff researchers and the general public. All documentation can be used for publication of studies on special subjects such as construction or conservation techniques, and dictionaries of special terms.

The address form provides basic information on all historical monuments, movable and immovable. Other products of the system include the collected detailed recording forms of the five separate inventories as well as the attached photographs, maps, drawings and additional supporting documentation such as photogrammetric records. The Archaeologic Map with its unified code of symbols is the prototype for a complex map of the entire country which will graphically depict all historical monuments.

Summary/Evaluation

The objectives of the Polish system are ambitious—the identification, documentation and protection of all historical and cultural monuments. Emphasis is placed on documentation leading to planned preservation by integrating this protection within the industrial and economic development of the country.

The Historical Monuments Documentation Centre provides organization, planning and supervision as well as the central file for all inventory documentation collected within the system. All information is objective and factual and revised to be up to date. Only the scope of the architectural survey is selective; all others are comprehensive. Reference citations including place of storage and call marks are most complete. Alphabetic-colour codes are useful for manual files.

Unfortunately the constant use of the term 'monuments' for both architecture and works of art is confusing. The separate inventory formats used for building exteriors and their important interior features are unwieldy. Computerization is still under development. On the detailed inventory sheets paragraphs may hide information. Long text statements preclude any easy eventual computerization. The terser responses on the address form are easier to read as well as to code; the pre-printed answers and graphic symbols for archaeology are the easiest.

Question analysis

An analysis of the kinds of information asked on the cover sheet for the Cities Inventory and on the address form and inventory sheet for the Monuments Inventory follows. All forms are of standard-sized A4 cardboard; answers are generally typed in text statements or paragraphs. Analysis is by category and not by question sequence on each form. For a question-by-question comparison of these Polish forms with the other systems see Part Three.

IDENTIFICATION/LOCATION

Both the address form and the inventory sheet identify the kind of object, and any name which may modify it, and ask whether the entry is demolished in the same question. The inventory sheet further describes present and original use of this monument. All three forms state the present Voivodship and locality. Both the cover sheet and

inventory sheet cite previous locality names such as popular place-names in common use among the local populations, or original German names for northern and western territories. Former administrative jurisdictions prior to 1 June 1975, when districts became communities, are given on both the address form and inventory sheet as are full street addresses which are to be checked on the spot. Also under 'street address' any previous name of the street is cited and relative distance to a road or nearby landmark if the object is outside a settlement. The inventory sheet provides legal address precision by referencing the mortgage register number and, in separate questions, the owner and his address, and the user and his address.

SIGNIFICANCE/DESIGNATION

No level of significance is cited on any form. However, the address fom is completed for all items considered to possess historical value. Both the address form and the Inventory Sheet note if the entry is enrolled in the official Register of Historical Monuments, its number and date of enrolment.

DATE/HISTORY

Both the address form and inventory sheet state the 'time of erection'. Known dates are given in arabic numerals while approximate dates are written in text within a quarter of a century. Only the inventory sheet asks historical questions. Authors, history of the object and style definition are all combined in one question. A second question, building works and conservation, defines the campaigns, scope of work, dates and who did the work as well as referencing any available documentation.

DESCRIPTION

The address form asks about material only. The inventory sheet provides one general question on description which covers situation, material and construction, plan, architectural mass, interiors, exteriors, furnishings and installations. Separate questions further describe cubic dimensions and usable floor area.

CONSERVATION/RESTORATION/PRESERVATION

Entries on the address form may 'deserve to be subjected to a conservator's care'. The cover sheet references the conservation record, date and number and, separately, any development plan. The inventory sheet asks for the state of preservation in one general question; this is the condition of foundations, walls, vaults, floors, rafters, roofing, furnishings and installations. A separate question notes the type and scope of conservation measures urgently needed. Earlier conservation is described in the question, building works and conservation.

DOCUMENTATION/REFERENCE

The address form notes citations in the *List of Historic Monuments, Catalogue of Ancient Objects*, and whether the entry is provided with a separate inventory sheet. The cover sheet cross-references the file number, archaeological data, the development plan and historical or town-planning studies. Also, a separate table of contents for the file is provided, and collected within the file are maps, photographs of historical maps and photographs of town-planning features.

The inventory sheet cites literature references. Other non-held illustrative sources are noted by type, place of storage and negative number. Similarly, archival materials notes the call marks and storage place for additional records concerning the object. Attached to the front of the inventory sheet is a map showing the location at a scale of 1:25,000 for town buildings or a sketch at 1:250 or 1:500 approximate scale for rural buildings. Also attached are plans at 1:100, 1:200 or 1:400 marked with basic measurements, scale and north. At least one 6 × 9 cm black-and-white photograph is also attached citing photographer's name, date and storage place for negatives.

Both the cover sheet and the inventory sheet have remarks for additional information. On the inventory sheet cross-references to other forms are cited under this question.

SYSTEMATIZATION

Recording record

The inventory sheet lists the names of the photographer, preparer and checker of the form as well as the dates of preparation.

Systematics

Across the top of the address form and the inventory sheet alpha-colour codes display varied information for manual use. The inventory sheet includes a blank for an eventual computerization number.

Appendix

ORIGINAL QUESTION SEQUENCE
TRANSLATED (FORM PL1)

Address Form
Object
Address
   Locality

Voivodship
Community
Street
Time of erection
Material
Former administrative jurisdiction
No. in Register of Historical Monuments
Documentation available:
   Provided with Inventory Sheet
   Mentioned in List of Historical Monuments
   Mentioned in Catalogue of Ancient Objects

ORIGINAL QUESTION SEQUENCE
TRANSLATED (FORM PL2)

File Cover Sheet

   Locality
   Voivodship
   Previous name(s)
   Administrative status
   Seat of local authorities
   File No.
   Date and No. of opinion by conservator
   No. of relevant conservator's records
   Historical and town-planning surveys
   Archaeological data
   Development plan
   Table of contents
   Remarks

ORIGINAL QUESTION SEQUENCE
AND TRANSLATION (FORM PL3)

	Inventory Sheet
Nr	Number
1. Obiekt	Object
2. Czas powstania	Time of erection
3. Miejscowość	Locality
4. Adres	Address
Nr hipoteczny	No. of mortgage register
5. Przynależność administracyjna	Administrative jurisdiction
Województwo	Voivodship
Gmina	Community
6. Poprzednie nazwy miejscowości	Previous locality names
7. Przynależność administracyjna przed 1.VI.1975	Administrative jurisdiction before 1 June 1975
Województwo	Voivodship
Powiat	Community
8. Właściciel i jego adres	Owner and his address
9. Użytkownik i jego adres	User and his address
10. Rejestr zabytków	Register of historical monuments
Nr. Data	No. Date

11. Zdjecia, plan sytuacyjny, rzuty — Photographs, situation, plans

12. Autorzy, historia obiektu, określenia stylu — Authors, history of object, style definition

13. Opis, etc. — Description, etc.

14. Kubatura — Cubic capacity

15. Powierzchnia uzytkowa — Usable floor area

16. Przeznaczenie pierwotne — Original usage

17. Uzytkowanie obeene — Present usage

18. Prace budowlane i konserwatorskie, etc. — Building works and conservation, etc.

19. Stan zachowania, etc — State of preservation

20. Najpilniejsze postulaty konserwatorskie — Type and scope of conservation measures

21. Akta archiwalne, etc. — Archival materials, etc.

22. Bibliografia — Literature references

23. Zródla ikonograficzne i fotografie — Illustrative sources and photography

24. Uwagi rózne — Remarks

25. Wypelnil — Prepared by

26. Sprawdzil — Checked by

Zambia (ZM)

Zambia National Site Index

Based on information supplied by
N. M. Kataneka, Director, National Monuments
Commission, and Robin Derricourt, ex-Director

Discussion

OBJECTIVES AND STATISTICS

The Zambia National Sites Index is operated as one of the duties of the National Monuments Commission. The Index serves: (a) to guide in the legal protection of sites; (b) to guide in the public administration related to sites; (c) to assist the research and information service of the National Monuments Commission and associated institutions; (d) to aid field research in archaeology and history; and (e) to assist international researchers as a published reference source.

Both legally protected and unprotected sites are recorded. Non-archaeological sites are 'unprotected'. All sites with human occupation before 1890 are 'protected'. Some sites are 'declared' national monuments.

Begun in 1974, the main effort was completed in 1976 with the publication of the *Classified Index of Archaeological and Other Sites in Zambia*[1] which included 1,543 sites.

STAFF

Systematic recording for the Index was done by the staff of the National Monuments Commission over a two-year period from available known sources generally without further field work. Updating the Index is a continuous process. Recorded errors are noted by users and corrected. New discoveries of sites and finds, which are required under Zambian law to be reported to the National Monuments Commission, are periodically entered into the system.

1. National Monuments Commission, *A Classified Index of Archaeological and Other Sites in Zambia* (ed. by R. M. Derricourt, rev. by E. Maluma), Livingstone, National Monuments Commission, 1978.

CRITERIA

The Index is intended to be comprehensive for known archaeological sites and localities containing chance finds, and selective for the most important historical, geological and traditional sites or areas of natural beauty. Selection is based on existence in the available known sources.

The variable and selective nature of the sources does not provide a standard level of reliability for the data. Changing and duplicate place-names cause confusion and some sites may be listed twice. For entries based on hearsay, without supporting information, the term 'unconfirmed' is used in the question of status.

METHOD

Category and site type

Basic to the Zambia National Sites Index is the division of all entries into separate questions for category and type. The five categories are: natural, geological, archaeological, historical and traditional. Natural sites are non-built; geological sites are palaeontological; archaeological means pre-colonial in date; historical means colonial or post-colonial; and traditional sites have importance for religion or local oral history but no visible features or finds.

For the natural category there are three types (waterfalls, non-archaeological caves and other); for traditional there are two types (traditional site and cave, traditional); for geological, three types (hard-rock fossils, fossilwood, and Quaternary fossils); for archaeology, twenty-four types (including settlement, fortified village, burial, open and sedimentary sites, various kinds of caves and finds); and for historical five types (administrative post, church/mission, monument, cemetery/

89

grave, and historical other). Thus, the few architectural site types are listed under the historical category and are colonial or post-colonial in date.

The site record card

Information is recorded in English on the site record card. Definitions of some questions are given in 'Notes on Entries' in the *Classified Index of Archaeological and Other Sites in Zambia*. No handbook or lexicon is available.

The 5 × 8 inch (127 × 203 mm) card asks twelve questions for computerization and ten non-computerized on the reverse. All questions (unnumbered) are pre-printed with blank spaces (not lines) below. Answers are written in text and, if computerized, also coded into boxes. By this method of pre-printing questions and answering in text as well as numeric codes, the completed card is immediately readable as well as ready to be punched on to computer tape.

For the questions 'category' and 'status', where five or six answers are standardized, each is preprinted on the form to be underlined. For the questions Publications, Excavations and C14 dates, a 'none' or 'yes' choice is possible. If 'none' is correct, it is written in the blank and '0' is entered into the code box. A 'yes' answer is described in full but only the fact that information exists (coded by 1) is computerized.

COMPUTERIZATION

Data processing is provided by the staff of the Data Processing Unit, Ministry of Finance. Entry length is fixed at 53 spaces. Entry for site name is in free text; all other questions are alpha-numeric codes. Print-out is the standard 132-space line. Province, category, status, periods and site type print out as easily readable keywords. Map co-ordinates, museum objects and file reference numbers remain as numerics. A '±' signifies additional references for objects and files.

PRODUCTS AND USERS

Products of the Zambia system include special computer listings, the manual file of completed site record cards and the *Classified Index of Archaeological and Other Sites in Zambia*. The published Index is distributed and used by international archaeologists.

The site record card file in the offices of the National Monuments Commission contains additional uncomputerized information for many of the sites. This may be consulted by students and scholars on request. Users of the system include the staffs of the National Monuments Commission and the Livingstone Museum as well as archaeological researchers.

Summary/Evaluation

The Zambia National Sites Index has many strengths. The site record card can be read manually and is a convenient size. Information is basic and controlled responses are easy to compare. There is a continuous programme of correction and expansion of the Index as errors are found by users and new sites added.

Periodization of dates allows for uncertainties. Data collection from available known sources avoided time-consuming and expensive field surveying while the use of 'unconfirmed' and 'confirmed' status clearly grade the reliability of the information. This is an operating and proven computer method which is easily updated.

Nevertheless, there are weaknesses in the Index. It is mainly archaeological with few architectural questions. There are no photographs or manual for the system. Unnumbered pre-printed questions on the site record card at first glance appear disorganized. Because it was based on known sources without a site visit, the Index data is not necessarily correct, nor was it collected at one particular time.

Question analysis

An analysis of the kinds of information asked on the Zambia Site Record Card follows. The analysis is by category and not by question sequence on the form. For a question-by-question comparison of these Zambian questions contrasted with the other systems, see Part Three.

IDENTIFICATION/LOCATION

Province, site name and latitude/longitude co-ordinates locate and identify the entry. Site name utilizes the official approved spelling unless another has been used in source publications. If necessary, indicators, such as A, B, etc., distinguish parts of sites with the same name. Alternate site names are written but not computerized. Co-ordinates provide degrees and minutes for south and east geographical axes and are computerized, while the map sheet reference is only cited. Two additional questions particularize location but are not computerized. Position/directions describes the direction and mileage from the nearest crossroads, track or recognizable landmark. Farm/chief/town further specify the locale. Two separate questions, 'category' and 'site type', classify the entry by broad kind of site category and particular type of site.

SIGNIFICANCE/DESIGNATION

The level of legal protection is listed under 'status'. Sites may be declared (national monuments), protected (having human occupation before 1890), unprotected or destroyed.

DATE/HISTORY

Archaeological and historical sites are dated by period. Up to four periods may be combined for any entry. If carbon-14 dates have been obtained, this is noted in a separate question. Sites associated with religion or local oral history are classified under the category, Traditional.

DESCRIPTION

Two non-computerized questions provide a general description of the site as well as a description of any finds associated with the site. If a site is represented by specimens in the Livingstone Museum collection, the object's accession number is recorded. If there is more than one such assemblage, this fact is noted. Only one museum object number is computerized.

CONSERVATION/RESTORATION/PRESERVATION

No question specifies this category. The actual condition of the site may be described in 'other information' which is non-computerized.

DOCUMENTATION/REFERENCE

Bibliographic information is given in 'publications'. Full citations are written but only the fact that a publication exists is computerized. References to the files of either the National Monuments Commission or the Livingstone Museum are cited by number. However, the file reference is not necessarily given if the site has been published. If there is more than one file, this fact is noted. If excavations have been made, complete references are cited, but only the fact that excavations are known is computerized. 'Other information' is an uncomputerized question for additional data.

SYSTEMATIZATION

Recording record

'Source/informant', an uncomputerized question, asks from where information was gathered, or by whom. Under 'status' the term 'unconfirmed' is applied to material or sites without adequate supporting information. Sites with adequate information are 'confirmed findspots'.

Systematics

Province and site name are repeated on both sides of the site record card for easier manipulation.

Appendix

ORIGINAL QUESTION SEQUENCE
(FORM ZM)
Site Record Card

Computerized questions
Province
Site name
Co-ordinates
Category
    Natural
    Geological
    Traditional
    Archaeological
    Historical
Status
    Declared
    Protected
    Confirmed findspot
    Destroyed
    Unconfirmed
    Unprotected
Periods
Site type
Museum objects
File refs.
Publications
Excavations
C.14 dates

Uncomputerized questions
Province
Site name
Map
Farm/chief/village
Alternate site names
Position/directions
Description of site
Finds
Other information
Source/informant

Part Three

Question comparison

Introduction

Inventorying the international cultural heritage is not a simple procedure of storing homogeneous facts. This is evident from the discussion of each system's methodology in Part Two. Diversity is the rule. Different countries' various methods for recording their heritage resources and interrogating those resources manifestly express their national cultural individuality.

Outline of question categories and topics

The actual questions that systems ask and how they ask them are at the heart of the problem of surveying cultural property. To find a common denominator among the eleven systems, the actual questions asked by each have been taken from the system description and placed within another framework superimposed by this Manual—the 'Outline of question categories and topics'. The 'Outline' is divided into seven thematic categories (in turn subdivided into topics) which accommodate the information elicited by all of the 600-plus questions asked by the eleven systems in six languages on the twenty-three different forms chosen for analysis here.

Keyed to the categories and topics of the 'Outline' is the detailed question analysis carried out by a series of twenty-six analytic charts. Every one of the 600 or so questions finds a place in these charts. Some questions which span several topics may be mentioned more than once.

All questions are identified in the left-hand column by country of origin and form (FR, PL3) on which the question was asked. (For an identification of the systems analysed, see p. 17.) In the centre column the questions are printed in English, either the original or translated. When information was provided in a language other than English, it is given in the right-hand column

for comparison. Also in this right-hand column are listed (in parentheses) the number of each question on its original form for cross-reference with the sequential question list appended to the individual system description in Part Two. Not all systems, however, follow the desirable practice of numbering questions.

Following each analytic chart the reader can compare what questions the various systems ask (or omit) within the twenty-six different topics. In any case, the individual questions can be traced back to their original national context in Part Two which may help clarify the special, local concerns that often motivate survey inquiry.

Question Typology (p. 136)

In order to provide an overview of all the question categories and topics, a question typology assembles, by category, the cosmopolitan cross-section of question types utilized by the systems and individually discussed within the analytic charts. Based on the author's opinion, these question types are ranked according to importance of their information for any potential inventory of immovable cultural property.

One type of information, called 'primary' on the Question Typology, should be basic and universal to virtually all systems regardless of cultural context, objectives or budget. This skeletal information is enriched by 'secondary' questions that usually reflect each system's local preoccupations and objectives. A third type of question, 'optional', may be employed by certain systems but in practice might lead to a point of diminishing returns in system productivity when the manpower needed to collect it accurately is balanced against its ultimate utility. The last column of the Question Typology, 'other', indicates when information may warrant profes-

sional staff recording, special updating procedures or the attachment of copies of documents or
photographs.

SYNTHESIS GRID (p. 141)

This final chart presents a graphic image of the
600-plus questions arranged on a coordinate grid
in such a way that the reader can see at once the
total distribution pattern of questions by system
and form, category and topic.

Outline
of question categories
and topics

	Analytic Chart No.
1. Identification/location	
A. Name	1A
B. Typology and use	1B
C. Address	1C
D. Cartographic co-ordinates and property registration	1D
E. Ownership	1E
2. Significance/Designation	
A. Importance	2A
B. Official designation and other legalities	2B
3. Date/History	
A. Date	3A
B. Historical commentary	3B
C. Authorship	3C
4. Description	
A. Area and setting	4A
B. Site and structure: magnitude	4B
C. Site and structure: general description	4C
D. Site and structure: style	4D

	Analytic Chart No.
E. Site and structure: material and technique	4E
F. Site and structure: construction elements	4F
G. Site and structure: immovable features	4G
H. Site and structure: movable features	4H
5. Conservation/Restoration/Preservation	5
A. Present condition	
B. Past work	
C. Future perspectives	
6. Documentation/Reference	
A. Published bibliography	6A
B. Files and reports	6B
C. Maps, plans and drawings	6C
D. Photographs	6D
E. Other information	6E
7. Systematization	
A. Recording record	7A
B. Systematics	7B

1. Identification/location

A. Name

AR12	Name	Denominación (9,8)
CA	Name(s) of building	Nom(s) du bâtiment(–)
CA	(Certainty code)	
FR	Titles—names	Titres—appellations (10)
FR	Type of user	Genre du destinataire (1030)
IN12	Name of monument/site	(1,4)
IT1	Name under *oggetto*	Oggetto
JP123	Name	
MX1	Name of church	Advocación
MX1	Name of religious order	Orden monástica original
MX2	Name of monument/place	Nombre
MA1	Name of monument/site	Nom du monument ou du site
MA23	Name	Dénomination
NYC	Present name	(22)
NYC	Original name	(23)
NYC	Complex name	(24)
PL12	Name under 'object'	Obiekt (–,1)
ZM	Site name	
ZM	Alternate site name	

DISCUSSION

This topic discusses present names for each entry, past names and questions which modify the names. All systems give the actual name of each entry, but only some have a separate question for that information. Both Poland and Italy include the names (past and present) under the object type. For example, Poland cites 'palace, called Krolikarnia' and Italy *'forte di S.Giorgio'*.

Many systems provide for alternative and/or past names. Canada does not enter the names into the main data base but has a separate computer file of names and location codes. Canada also notes the level of certainty for the name according to whether staff or non-staff did the research. In New York City the present name, original name and name of the complex are all asked for and computerized. Zambia computerizes only the name of the site but records alternative site names as well.

France and Mexico modify the name by specifying the type of user (*genre du destinataire*) or particular religious order (*orden monástica original*). Thus, for Mexico the church named 'San Ignacio' can be modified by 'Jesuitas'.

The full name of the entry as it is known at the time of recording is primary information and must be collected. Original and alternative names might also be recorded. The precision possible with the use of a modifier or a certainty code is worth considering.

B. Typology and use

ANALYTIC CHART 1B

AR12	Inventory number	Número de inventario (1,1)
AR1	Present use	Utilización existente (13)
AR1	Proposed use	Utilización propuesta (13)
AR1	Level of adaptability	Grado de adaptabilidad (19)
CA	Present use(s)	Usage actuel (6)
CA	State	État (9)
CA	Original use(s)	Usage initial (7)
CA	Associated use(s)	Usage apparenté (8)
FR	Denomination	Dénomination (1010)
FR	Regional typology	Typologie régionale (70)
FR	Constituent parts	Parties constituents (1060)
FR	Present use	Destination actuelle (10)
IN1	Utilization	(14)
IN2	Used for religious purposes	(6)
IT1	Object	Oggetto
IT1	Original use	Destinazione originaria
IT1	Actual use	Uso attuale
IT2	Building types and distribution	Individuazione dei tipi edilizi ed analisi della loro distribuzione
IT3	(Past) uses	Destinazioni
IT4	Typology	Tipologia
IT4	Actual use	Destinazioni d'uso
JP1	Structure	
JP2	Kind	
MX12	Type	Tipo
MA1	Type-order number	Type-n° d'ordre
MA23	(Type-order) number	N°
MA23	Present state	État actuel
MA3	Evolution of use	Evolution subie
MA3	Present use	Utilisation actuelle
MA3	Proposed use	Utilisation proposée
MA3	Possible use	Utilisation possible
NYC	Present use(s)	(14–15)
NYC	Original use(s)	(16–17)
PL13	Object	Obiekt (–1)
PL3	Present usage	Uzytkowanie obeene (17)
PL3	Original usage	Przeznaczenie pierwotne (16)
ZM	Category	
ZM	Site type	

DISCUSSION

For many systems, Type or Use is the basic question. Type is the 'essence' of the entry which, for architecture, may be what it was built to be. It need not be the same as either its original use or its actual use (what it was first used for or what it is presently used for). Type for Argentina, France, Italy, Mexico, Morocco, Poland and Zambia is the basic entry question. Many of these systems also have separate questions for use (present, past or original, and future). For New York City and Canada, 'original use' provides the type.

France combines the general category of type with the specific kind in one question called *Dénomination*. The five separate categories (*Collectifs, Ensembles, Edifices, Edicules,* and *Parties*) each include particular types. For example, the category *Edifice* contains the specific *cathédrale*. In addition, separate questions ask about regional typology and constituent parts or uses not implied by the denomination. Present use is also given.

Italy identifies the kind of object (*oggetto*) and also asks for both the actual use and original use. For urban sectors the types of constructions as well as their past and present uses are described.

Morocco, for both monuments and sites, codes the type and numeric sequence within that type (*type-numéro d'ordre*). For monuments the present use and state as well as proposed and possible uses are given in four separate questions.

Argentina will code type into the inventory number. In addition, for monuments the actual use, proposed use, and level of future adaptability are given.

Mexico codes the type for both religious architecture and monument/place. Within the monument/place list, only two types imply use—church in use (*iglesia en servicio*) and church with other function (*iglesia con otra fonción*).

Poland identifies the kind of object as well as the present use and original uses in separate questions.

For Zambia two questions describe type; five categories of site modify thirty-eight site types. No question is asked for use.

For Canada and New York City the original use serves as the basic type question. Present use is asked as well.

Abandonment or disuse may also be noted. The existence of an abandoned building is cited by Canada in the question 'state' and by Morocco in the question '*état actuel*'. New York City includes abandoned as a use, as does Italy where abandoned or disused buildings are described as 'none' (*nessuno*).

RECOMMENDATIONS

Typology is a primary question and must be included in every inventory. For architecture, the original purpose for which a structure was built may also be its type. However, this is separate from the original use to which it may have been put or the present use and future use which might be collected. Regional variations in terminology are also useful.

C. Address
ANALYTIC CHART 1C

AR12	Province	Provincia (2,2)
AR12	Region	Región (3,3)
AR12	ENCOTEL	ENCOTEL (4,4)
AR12	District	Circunscripción (5,5)
AR12	Section	Sección (6,6)
AR12	Block	Manzana (7,7)
AR12	Specific address	Ubicación (8,9)
CA	Province/territory	Province/territoire
CA	Town	Ville
CA	County	Comté
CA	District	District
CA	Township	Canton
CA	Street	Rue
CA	Building number	N° du bâtiment
FR	Region	Région (1130)
FR	Department	N° dépt (1130)
FR	Canton	Canton (1130)
FR	Commune	Commune (1130)
FR	Place name or urban sector	Lieu-dit ou secteur urbain (30)
FR	Address	Adresse (40)
FR	Specifics	Précisions sur localisation (1140)
IN1	State	
IN12	District	(–,2)
IN12	Locality	(2,3)
IN1	Subdivision	(4)
IN1	Approach	(5)
IT1234	Region	Regione
IT1234	Province	Provincia
IT12	Commune	Commune
IT2	Neighbourhood	Rione
IT2	Delimiting streets	Via di delimitazione
IT34	Delimiting streets	. . . compreso tra via
IT1	Address	Luogo

ANALYTIC CHART 1C (*contd.*)

JP123	Location	
MX12	State	Nombre del estado
MX1	Municipality	Municipio
MX12	Town	Población
MX1	Parish	Parroquia
MX2	Address	Localización
MA12	Province	Province
MA3	Province, main place	Province, chef-lieu
MA123	Circle	Cercle
MA1	Urban commune or rural douar	Commune urbaine ou rurale (douar)
MA2	Commune	Commune
MA1	Town	Ville
MA3	Town, commune	Ville, commune
MA2	Place	Lieu-dit
MA3	Quarter or place	Quartier, lieu-dit
NYC	Borough	(1)
NYC	Community	(10)
NYC	Street	(5)
NYC	Numeric address	(6–7)
NYC	Also known as street	(8)
NYC	Also known as numeric	(9)
PL123	Voivodship	Województwo (–,–,5)
PL123	Locality	Miejscowość (–,–,3)
PL23	Previous locality names	Poprzednie nazwy miejscowośći (–,6)
PL13	Community	Gmina (–,5)
PL1	Street	
PL3	Address	Adres (4)
PL13	Former administrative jurisdiction	Przynalezność administracyjna (–,7)
PL2	Administrative status	
PL2	Seat of local authorities	(–)
ZM	Province	
ZM	Farm/chief/town	
ZM	Position/directions	

DISCUSSION

As a rule, location is expressed by means of a given country's geographic-administrative terminology. In general this information descends from the broadest area (region, province, state, etc.) down to a specific address in five or six questions. For the specific address some systems utilize actual street locations or include distance from known landmarks.

Japan, an exception, asks only for location, by which is meant the city, town or village. India, under approach, cites the nearest railway station and authority for reserving accommodation. Poland includes non-official or popular place-names under previous locality. In addition, the former administrative jurisdiction as well as the present is given. Zambia computerizes province but records farm/chief/town as well.

Some of the systems give actual street addresses: Argentina, Canada (for urban structures), Mexico and Poland. For France, street addresses are not necessary for major buildings but are indispensable for houses. If an address does not exist an artificial address number is assigned. Specifics includes 'forbidden addresses' where private owners refuse to let their addresses be listed. New York City provides the possibilities of two different street addresses. Italy gives street addresses for individual buildings but for urban sectors the neighbourhood and streets delimiting the block are cited.

Mexico, Poland and Zambia may include distance in the specific address. For Mexico the mileage to the nearest town and/or suburb is acceptable as well as a numeric address. Poland for rural entries records the distance to the nearest locality. For Zambia the question position/directions includes mileage from the nearest cross-roads or town.

RECOMMENDATIONS

Address is a primary question. The more precise the information, the better the identification of each entry. By using five geographic-administrative divisions, plus the specific address, each entry should be located. Since names of administrative areas and places can change over time, alternative and common names may be worth collecting. For an urban structure facing on two streets the alternative address might be collected. Mileage, though better than no location, is vague.

D. Cartographic co-ordinates and property registration

ANALYTIC CHART 1D

AR	——	
CA	Map number	N° de la carte
CA	Building number	N° du bâtiment sur la carte
CA	Concession number	N° de concession
CA	Lot number	N° de lot
FR	Cartographic co-ordinates	Co-ordonnées cartographiques (1170)
FR	Cadastral reference	Références cadastrales (50)
FR	Displaced conserved parts	Edifice ou ensemble de conservation (50)
IN1	Lat. N. long. E.	(3)
IN1	Survey sheet number	(3)
IT1234	Cadastre folio parcel	Catasto folio n. part. nm.
IT2	Topographic co-ordinates	Riferimenti topografia
IT34	Parcel	Particella
JP13	Range	
MX	——	
MA1	Exact co-ordinates	Localisation exacte
MA2	Exact location and limits of zones	Situation exacte et limites de zones
MA3	Exact location	Situation exacte
MA3	Cadastre	Cadastre
NYC	Block	(2)
NYC	Lot	(3)
NYC	Part	(4)
PL3	Mortgage register number under 'address'	Nr hipoteczny (4)
ZM	Co-ordinates	
ZM	Map	

DISCUSSION

Cartographic co-ordinates and legal property registration may be recorded to add precision to location information. India, Zambia, France and Morocco all cite established cartographic references. India asks for latitude and longitude and specifies the survey sheet used. Zambia records degrees and minutes south and east but only refers to the map sheet in a separate non-computerized question. Both France and Morocco use the Lambert zones for topographic accuracy. They also cite legal cadastral references.

Italy always cites cadastral references including folio and parcel number for each entry. For urban sectors, the parcel of the block becomes the identifier for a series of questions. Precise topographic co-ordinates are also given for the urban sector. Copies of the appropriate maps are included as supportive documentation.

For rural recording, Canada uses National Topographic System maps where possible, but each map is renumbered with a unique CIHB system number. Each recorded building on the map is numbered in sequence as recorded. The legal concession number and lot number are asked for but not computerized.

Japan cites only the legal lot reference. New York City uses the legal borough, block, lot and parcel (part) reference as listed in the Sanborn Landbook but records no actual map sheet number. Poland cites the legal address reference in the Mortgage Register.

RECOMMENDATIONS

Legal registration and cartographic co-ordinates are both secondary information which might be recorded to add precision to address locations. If convenient, established methods should be used for mapping as in the French and Indian systems, for example, but individualized methods like Canada's can prove quite expedient. For any cartographic system, however, the map sheet number as well as the plotted grid reference need to be identified.

Legal registration refers to the official land-holdings and is useful for specifying particular properties. Cadastral references used by France, Italy and Morocco are paralleled by the Japanese 'range' and the New York City 'block, lot and parcel'.

E. Ownership

ANALYTIC CHART 1E

AR	——	
CA	Present owner	Propriétaire actuel
CA	Address of owner	Adresse du propriétaire
CA	Tenant	Locataire
CA	Original owner or tenant	Propriétaire ou locataire d'origine
FR	Ownership under 'legal status'	'Situation juridique' (1550)
IN12	Ownership	(12,5)
IN2	Record of classification	(17)
IT14	Ownership	Proprietà
IT3	(Past) ownership	Proprietà
JP12	Owner, name and address	
JP2	Possessor, name and address	
MA23	Owner; responsible office	Propriétaire; administration responsable
MX1	Owner of church under 'religious order'	'Orden monástica original'
NYC	——	
PL3	Owner and his address	Wlaściciel i jego adres (8)
PL3	(Type of owner)	
PL3	User and his address	Uzytkownik i jego adres (9)
PL3	Original owner under 'history of object'	'Historia obiektu' (12)
ZM	——	

DISCUSSION

The type of owner, name of present owner and tenant, as well as past or original owner may all be specified. France, India and Italy ask for the type of owner, whether private or governmental. France includes this information under Legal Status. India, for governmental ownership notes if the property was a gift or bequest and attaches a copy of the 'instrument' to the record. For governmental ownership the responsible agency is cited both by India (recorded classification) and Morocco (*administration résponsable*).

Canada, Japan and Poland provide owner's name as well as any tenant, possessor or user. In addition Poland codes the type of owner for office use. Morocco gives only owner's name. Mexico, for private churches, identifies the hacienda under Religious Order. Canada, Italy and Poland ask for past owners, Canada by name, Italy by type. Poland records original owner under History of the Object. Although the CIHB is computerized, none of the ownership information is entered into the computer.

RECOMMENDATIONS

Ownership type is secondary information that might be recorded. It is less variable than the actual names and addresses of owners which needs to be kept current in order to be accurate. Present and past owners' names and addresses as well as tenants or users are considered optional. All might be referenced in another file. Copies of any deeds or bequests are also optional information.

2. Significance/ designation

A. Importance

AR1	Level of importance	Grado de valor (18)
CA	——	
FR	Interest in the work	A signaler intérêt de l'œuvre(1590)
IN1	Brief history, importance and outstanding features	(6)
IT	——	
JP	——	
MX	——	
MA	——	
NYC	Significance	(21)
PL	——	
ZM	——	

DISCUSSION

Only Argentina, France, India and New York City cite the level of importance, interest or significance of each entry. India combines importance in a general descriptive paragraph with history and features. Argentina asks for importance only for monuments. France can signal if an entry should be protected by the Monuments Historiques or, for destroyed works, should have been protected. New York City combines levels of significance in one question with levels of designation.

RECOMMENDATIONS

For any system which deals with both legally protected and non-protected entries, and is used as a tool for protection selection, importance is a primary question. In New York City, for example, all churches are not of equal significance. One objective of the UCRS is to establish designation priorities based on importance. Nevertheless, the whole question of judgement is a thorny one and needs a well-trained eye, generally professional. Subjective judgements of merit may cause offence to some users of the system. It is interesting to note that the first edition (1970) of the CIHB included levels of significance and the present fourth edition (1979) has apparently dropped this potentially sensitive question.

For systems which deal with both legally protected and unprotected entries and are not used as a guide for selection, importance is a secondary question. For systems where all entries are protected this is an optional question.

B. Official designation and other legalities

ANALYTIC CHART 2B

AR1	Level of present protection	Grado de protección existente (16)
AR1	Level of proposed protection	Grado de protección propuesta (17)
AR2	Extent of protection	Protección—extension (10)
AR2	Type of protection	Tipo de protección (11)
CA	Recognized historical site	Reconnu lieu historique (81)
FR	Legal status	Situation juridique (1550)
IN12	Authority, number and date of notification	(10,8)
IN1	Section and act	(11)
IN12	Agreement	(13,7)
IN1	Revenue	(15)
IT12	Decrees	Vincoli
JP123	Designation date	
JP1	Number of certificate	
JP23	Number of announcement	
JP23	Official criteria	
JP23	Explanation	
JP23	Alteration dates	
JP3	Preservation plan	
JP3	Regulations for preservation	
JP3	Related rules and regulations	
JP3	Measures taken by municipality	
MX	——	
MA1	Legal status	Statut foncier
MA1	Protection decision	Décision de protection
MA2	Present protection	Protection existant
MA2	Degree of protection	Degré de protection
MA2	Future protection	Protection prévue
MA3	Legal protection	Protection légale
MA3	Type of decision	Nature de la décision
MA123	Number	N°
MA123	Date	Date
NYC	Designation level under 'significance'	(21)
PL13	Register of historical monuments, number and date	Rejestr zabytków Nr data (–,10)
ZM	Status	

DISCUSSION

By designation is meant legal protection. Several systems cite only the level of protection; others specify the actual decrees by date, number, etc., and may attach copies of the texts. In addition to stating present designation, future levels may also be proposed.

Argentina, Canada, New York City and Zambia reference the level of protection. Argentina, for monuments, notes both the level of existing and proposed protection. For sites, the extent and type of protection are given. Canada records recognized historic sites at national, provincial, regional or municipal levels. New York City in the question called 'significance' also records the levels of municipal and federal landmark designation. Zambia provides the level of protection under 'status'. Sites may be declared (national monuments), protected, unprotected as well as confirmed findspots, unconfirmed, and destroyed.

Morocco, France, India, Italy, Japan and Poland reference the actual date and/or number of legal protection. Morocco cites present protection by type, date and number and proposes future protection. France, under the question 'situation juridique', notes the date on which entries were either classified or inscribed by the Monuments Historiques as well as ownership and museum storage. Poland gives the number and date of enrolment in the Register of Historic Monuments. Italy cites the legal decrees (vincoli) by number and date.

India gives the authority, number and date of the official notification and cites other legalities as well. If an agreement exists between the government and owner, it is noted. Any revenue from a lease or endowment is recorded. Copies of the Notification and Agreement are attached to the official record.

Japan has the most complete designation information. The date, designation number and number of the announcement in the official gazette are cited. Criteria for designation are given and explained. The term 'alteration' allows for future changes to historic site or preservation district designations. For districts many other legal regulations are cited by name and date. Full copies of the decrees are attached to the Ledger.

RECOMMENDATIONS

The level of designation or legal protection is primary information and must be recorded unless all the entries have the same designation. Designation levels change and should be kept current. This legal information should not be mixed with other data such as significance, ownership, etc.

The date and number of designation are secondary questions that might be recorded, as are the legal criteria by which designation was made, date of announcement, any agreement, as well as proposed or future designation. However, copies or texts of any decree are optional information that could be recorded.

3. Date/history

A. Date

AR1	Date of initiation	Fecha de inicio (11)
AR1	Date of completion	Fecha de terminación (12)
CA	Year(s) of construction	Année(s) de construction (1)
CA	Known or estimated	Données connues ou estimatives
CA	(Certainty code)	
CA	Year of demolition	Année de démolition (2)
CA	Known or estimated	Données connues ou estimatives
CA	(Certainty code)	
FR	Dating	Datation (1370)
FR	Destroyed under	
	'conservation'	'Conservation' (1510)
IN	——	
IT12	Chronology	Cronologia
IT3	Period	Epoca
JP1	Year or period	
MX1	Approximate date	Fecha aproximado
MX2	Approximate date	Año o siglo aproximado
MA1	Date	Date
MA3	Construction period	Epoque de construction
NYC	Original date	(25)
NYC	If estimated	(26)
NYC	Date of change	(27)
NYC	If estimated	(28)
PL13	Time of erection	Czas powstania (–,2)
PL13	Demolished under 'object'	'Obiekt' (–,1)
ZM	Periods	
ZM	C.14 dates	
ZM	Destroyed under 'status'	

DISCUSSION

Date citations are given as precise years, periods or centuries. Some systems provide only the year or periods; others give both. The kind of date may be distinguished by different citation formats such as Arabic numbers, Roman numerals or text. Accuracy statements may modify dates based on research or investigation. In addition the year of demolition or destruction may be recorded.

Argentina, Canada, and New York City record the numeric years. However, when computerized the years can be sorted into chronological periods. Argentina for monuments asks for the date of commencement and completion. Canada separates years in which construction commenced and was completed. New York City records one original date as well as one date of subsequent change, such as alteration.

Mexico and Zambia ask only for the period. Mexico codes the century third in Arabic numbers. For example, '16 3' represents the last third of the sixteenth century. Zambia names the relevant period. Up to four possibilities are allowed for each entry. An additional question records whether any Carbon-14 dates have been obtained.

Japan, France, Italy, Morocco and Poland give both years and periods. Japan, for 'treasures', notes either the year or period of construction. France allows for periodization to the nearest quarter century in text; also precise numeric years can be noted.

Italy, in the question '*cronologia*', cites both the century in Roman numerals and the years in Arabic numbers. For 'urban sectors' the relevant period for historic information is stated separately. Morocco computerizes either the A.D. or Hegira date in '+/−' numerics, while for monuments the construction period (*époque de construction*) is given. Poland writes in text the century of erection approximated to the nearest quarter and uses Arabic numbers for precise years.

Canada, France, and New York City modify dates with accuracy questions. France notes if the date is known by historical research. New York City distinguishes dates which are estimated; Canada specifies if dates are estimated or known by research and the reliability of that research.

Canada, France, New York City, Poland and Zambia provide demolition or destruction information. For buildings destroyed after recording Canada updates the year of demolition. New York codes demolition under year of (ultimate) change. France includes under conservation entries which are 'destroyed' as well as those which were 'destroyed after inventory'. Poland records demolished' under the question which identifies the object. Zambia notes 'destroyed' under 'status'. Neither France, Poland or Zambia date destruction or demolition.

RECOMMENDATIONS

Date is a primary question. Either or both the general chronological periods and the precise years must be collected (in separate questions). Since changes occur through time possibilities for multiple dates should always be provided. For architecture, dates of commencement, completion of the primary phase and subsequent changes might all be recorded. Destruction or demolition after recording is primary information which must be kept current. Accuracy or certainty questions modifying dates are secondary information.

B. Historical commentary

ANALYTIC CHART 3B

AR12	Evolution, chronology	Evolución, datos cronológicos (21,13)
CA	——	
FR	Historical commentary	Commentaire historique (60)
IN1	Brief history...	(6)
IT1	Construction events	Vicende costruttive
IT1	Urban events	Sistema Urbano
IT3	Historic events	Vicende storiche
IT4	Development phases	Fasi di sviluppo
JP1	First construction and history	
MX1	Legends and traditions	Legendas y tradiciones
MX1	Dates of festivals	Ferias y fiestas
MA23	History and popular traditions	Histoire et traditions populaires
MA3	Evolution	Evolution subie
NYC	Socio-historic significance	(76)
PL3	History of object	Historia obiektu (12)
PL3	Building works and conservation	Prace budowlane i konserwatorskie (18)
ZM	Traditional under 'category'	

DISCUSSION

Two general types of historical commentary are included. Some questions discuss the history of the building which may describe the construction campaign as well as subsequent phases of development. Others mention general associated history such as events, legends and traditions.

India combines (unspecified) history with importance and features in one question. Japan includes first construction with history in one question for National Treasures.

Construction history or building campaigns may be detailed as well as the history of the building itself. Both Argentina and Morocco include questions on evolution. Italy relates as construction events the historic, social, and economic history of each building. For urban sectors, the development phases are given. France describes building campaigns in the *Commentaire historique*. Poland describes under history of the object the part it played within the history of the town. A separate question records building works and conservation campaigns.

Associated events may also be noted. For New York City, socio-historic significance details matters of non-aesthetic importance such as birthplaces or battle sites. Italy, in the question

Sistema Urbano, relates urban or territorial events relevant to an individual building's history. The separate Historic Research Insert describes historic events for each parcel of an urban sector.

Zambia, Mexico and Morocco all cite local traditional history. Zambia classifies as Traditional those sites that have some importance in religion or local oral history. Mexico, for religious architecture, records the dates of fiestas and asks for but does not computerize related legends or traditions. Morocco collects history and popular traditions in one question for both monuments and sites.

RECOMMENDATIONS

Historical commentary, whether associated with actual events, legends or traditions or construction and development phases, is a secondary question that might be recorded.

Such information enriches the primary data and is fascinating as well as complex. It is perhaps the most difficult to organize and to restrict. The simplest appropriate organization may be by topic and short text paragraphs. If long paragraphs combine several topics, data tend to be lost.

C. Authorship
ANALYTIC CHART 3C

AR1	Chief of project	Proyectista (10)
CA	Architect	Architecte (3)
CA	(Certainty code)	
CA	Major builder or contractor	Entrepreneur principal ou constructeur (4)
CA	(Certainty code)	
CA	Engineer	Ingénieur (5)
FR	Authors	Auteurs (1310)
FR	Identification	Origine de l'identification (1320)
IN	——	
IT1	Author	Autore
JP	——	
MX	Constructor under 'religious order'	'Orden monástica original'
MA	——	
NYC	Primary architect	(29)
NYC	Of firm	(30)
NYC	Secondary architect	(31)
NYC	Of firm	(32)
PL3	Authors, history ...	Autorzy, historia obiektu ... (12)
ZM	——	

DISCUSSION

Authorship identifies the name(s) of the architect or firm, *maître d'œuvre*, sculptor or artist, builder or contractor, engineer, or even patron associated with the entry.

France, Italy and Canada all modify this question. France asks if the author is known by signature or historic research. Italy notes any attributions and Canada, with the certainty code, records the level or research which determined the name.

Poland includes author with the general question 'history of object'. The other systems provide separate questions for this information. Mexico uses the question 'religious order' to identify either the order or hacienda that sponsored construction of the church. However, this is not the actual builder or designer of the building. Canada differentiates between archi-tect, builder or contractor and engineer, and provides three separate answer possibilities for each. New York City allows two possibilities each for architect and architectural firm. France includes the *maître d'œuvre* as well as any sculptors or artists associated with the work. Argentina lists the *proyectista* for monuments only. Italy gives authors in chronological sequence.

RECOMMENDATIONS

Authorship is a secondary question for archi-tectural inventories. Possibilities should be provided for many names associated with each entry. Professional roles such as architect, master craftsman, etc., might also be distinguished. Accuracy or certainty modifying authorship is also a secondary question.

4. Description

A. Area and setting

ANALYTIC CHART 4A

AR	——	
CA	Property features	Caractéristiques de la propriété (78)
FR	Placement	Milieu d'implantation (1210)
FR	Importance for collective form	Importance du bordereau collectif (1410)
IN1	Topographical features	(8)
IN1	Area and boundary ...	(16)
IN1	Nature and extent of garden	(20)
IN1	Staff ...	(21)
IT1	Ambience	Rapport ambientali
IT2	Urban relationships by function	Correlazione urbanistiche par funzionali
IT2	Etymology of place names	Etimologia della toponomastica
IT2	Original urban plant ...	Impianto urbanistico originario
IT2	Division of land	Lottizzazione de impianto
IT2	Urbanistic relationships (of volumes)	Correlazione urbanistiche
JP1	Number of buildings (count)	
JP2	Custodian	
JP2	Acreage	
JP2	Number of lots	
JP3	City planning district	
JP3	Area	
JP3	Number of population	
JP3	Number of households	
JP3	Number of houses	
JP3	Number of buildings	
MX	——	
MA3	Setting and contents	Cadre et contenu
NYC	Property features	(65)
PL2	Historical and town-planning surveys	
PL3	Situation under 'description'	'Opis' ...(13)
ZM	Chief under 'farm/chief/town'	

DISCUSSION

Within this topic the area and the setting are discussed. This can include quantity or size and urbanistic relationships that describe the area as well as placement, property features and personnel which elaborate the setting.

Some information may be quantified as on the French form which counts for collectives how many entries were studied, noted and built. Japan asks for acreage and the quantity of lots which make up a historic site. For districts, the size of the area, total population, as well as numbers of households, buildings and houses are all enumerated.

Various urbanistic relationships are related by Italy, Japan and Poland. For Historic Cities and Towns, Poland cross-references other historical and town-planning surveys. Japan notes whether or not an area proposed by a municipality for historic district selection is within a City Planning District. Italy relates every urban sector to the rest of the city by present function. In addition, it describes successive changes in place names, functions and divisions of land as well as volumetric relationships between open and built-up areas.

For administrative purposes India, Japan and Zambia all mention personnel associated with the site. Zambia identifies the name of the tribal chief. For Historic Sites Japan records the custodian. India identifies the staff attached to the monument or site.

Many systems include information of the immediate placement, ambience or situation. France notes placement as either isolated or in an agglomeration, city or village. Italy describes the setting surrounding the building as urban, isolated or natural. Poland includes 'situation' in a general question on description; in towns all buildings are related to the historic town market. India, in separate questions, records topographical features, any garden attached to the monument as well as the area and boundary. Morocco describes the setting of a monument together with its contents (*cadre et contenu*). For National Treasures Japan counts the number of buildings which comprise the treasure. Canada and New York City identify individual property features such as fences or gates.

RECOMMENDATIONS

Descriptions of area and setting are secondary but useful questions. For an area or district the acreage, number of lots, population, and number of structures might all be counted. References may be made to planning information. Relationships between the area and the rest of the city may be described. Various information for the setting describing situation, features and personnel might all be recorded.

B. Site and structure: magnitude

ANALYTIC CHART 4B

AR	——	
CA	Massing of units	Groupement des unités (11)
CA	Plan	Plan (12)
CA	Wings	Ailes (13)
CA	Building dimension	Dimensions du bâtiment (14)
CA	Bays	Nombre de baies (16)
CA	Basement/foundation	Sous-sol/fondations (17)
FR	Plan	Plan (1420)
FR	Naves and floors	Vaisseaux et étages (1430)
FR	Exterior elevation	Élévation extérieure (1460)
FR	Dimensions	Dimensions (1490)
IN	——	
IT1	Plan	Pianta
IT1	Description	Descrizione
JP1	Area and height	
MX1	Atrium	Atrio
MX1	Crossing	Cruz atrial
MA	——	
NYC	Massing of structure	(33)
NYC	Visible units	(34–37)
NYC	Plot width	(38)
NYC	Plot depth	(39)
NYC	Building width	(40)
NYC	Building depth	(41)

ANALYTIC CHART 4B (*contd.*)

NYC	Storeys	(42)
NYC	Basement	(43)
NYC	Attic	(44)
NYC	Bays	(45)
NYC	Architectural composition	(68)
NYC	Elevation composition	(73)
NYC	Plan	(75)
PL3	Massing and plan under 'description'	'Opis' (13)
PL3	Cubic capacity	Kubatura (14)
PL3	Usable floor area	Powierzchnia uzytkowa (15)
ZM	——	

DISCUSSION

This topic considers the matter of magnitude for the Site and Structure by which is meant dimensions, plan shapes or types and elaborations of volume or mass.

Canada measures the depth and width of the building in metres. New York City details the building depth and width and the plot depth and width in feet. France provides dimensions only for *édicules* (constructions) and not *édifices* (buildings). Japan records the area of a National Treasure and includes height or other indications of size. In two separate questions Poland measures a building's cubic capacity as well as its usable floor area.

Plan type is specified by Canada, France, Italy and New York City. In addition, Canada asks for type of plan and whether wings have been added. For churches, Mexico records if there is an atrium (*atrio*) or a crossing (*cruz atrial*). Poland includes plan under the general question on description.

Further questions may elaborate the massing or volume of each structure. France, Canada and New York City count the number of floors or storeys. France details the exterior elevation. New York City specifies the elevational and architectural composition. New York and Canada count construction bays and record the basement type. New York mentions if there is an attic. Both Canada and New York describe the massing on the street; New York notes identical units or mirror images as well. Poland includes massing in the general question, Description. Italy combines levels, size and description of the street façade within the one question, *Descrizione*.

RECOMMENDATIONS

Descriptions of structural magnitude are secondary questions. Various information concerning linear or cubic dimensions, plan types and massing or volume such as the number of floors and façade composition might all be recorded. If dimensions are given standard units of measurement this should be noted.

C. Site and structure: general description

ANALYTIC CHART 4C

AR	——	
CA	——	
FR	——	
IN1	Outstanding features	(6)
IT	——	
JP	——	
MX	——	
MA23	Description	Description
MA3	Particular characteristics	Caractéristiques particulières
NYC	——	
PL3	Description	Opis (13)
ZM	Description of site	

DISCUSSION

India, Morocco, Poland and Zambia all ask general descriptive questions. India includes the outstanding features of the monument or site in one question which also covers brief history and importance. Morocco, for Monuments, asks unspecified *caractéristiques particulières* as well as *description* for Monuments and Sites. Zambia records description but does not computerize this information. Poland, in the single question called 'description', specifies situation, material and construction, plan, massing, exterior and interior, and furnishings.

RECOMMENDATIONS

General accounts of description are secondary questions which are not recommended. Descriptive information should not be combined in one question with other data such as history. Nor should description be unspecified. Questions that combine unrelated data or do not specify data, hide information. It then becomes necessary to read through the entire description in order to locate information describing, for example, the roof. Therefore, general unspecified descriptive accounts are not recommended.

D. Site and structure: style

ANALYTIC CHART 4D

AR	——	
CA	Style	Style (82)
FR	——	
IN	——	
IT	——	
JP1	Style	
MX	——	
MA	——	
NYC	Style	(18-21)
PL3	Style	Określenia Stylu (12)
ZM	——	

DISCUSSION

Few systems give stylistic descriptions. Japan specifies style only for National Treasures. Only staff record style in Canada. Poland includes style under history of object. New York City allows three possibilities of overall style for each entry plus the modification of many individual parts with their own style should they differ from the overall style.

RECOMMENDATIONS

Style is a secondary question. However, stylistic determinations need a well-trained eye, generally professional. This is not a question for volunteers. Since stylistic changes occur over time, several possibilities should be provided for each entry. Modifying various architectural parts or elements by their individual style is also useful.

It is interesting to note that the original edition of the CIHB (1970) did not ask about style. In the current fourth editio

E. Site and structure: material and technique

ANALYTIC CHART 4E

AR	——	
CA	Exterior bearing wall construction	Construction des murs porteurs extérieurs (30)
CA	Material of:	Matériau :
CA	basement/foundation wall	des murs de fondation (18)
CA	main exterior wall façade	principal du mur extérieur-façade (19–28)
CA	exterior wall material; other walls	des murs extérieurs; autres murs (29)
CA	roof surface	de la surface du toit (34)
CA	roof trim	de la garniture du toit (36, 38)
CA	chimney stacks	des souches de cheminée (45)
CA	window trims	garniture (50–52, 55–56)
CA	window sill	seuil de fenêtre (54)
CA	entrance trims	entrée principal—garniture (63–67)
CA	porch	porche (75)
FR	Material of total structure	Matériau de gros œuvre (1390)
FR	Material of roofing	Matériau de couverture (1400)
IN	——	
IT1	Wall construction	Techniche murarie
IT1	Subterranean structure	Strutture sotteranee
IT4	Construction technique	Techniche costruttive
MX	——	
MA3	Materials	Matériaux
NYC	Materials of façade	(46)
NYC	Façade material	(47)
NYC	Trim material	(100–999)
NYC	Surface coating	(67)
PL1	Material	
PL3	Material and construction technique under 'description'	'Opis' (13)
ZM	——	

DISCUSSION

Construction techniques as well as materials are discussed. Canada, Italy, New York City and Poland all specify construction technique. Italy includes materials with technique in the same questions.

Poland and Morocco ask about general materials. France specifies materials for the roof and those of the total work. Canada and New York City are most specific in detailing materials. Canada provides the materials of walls, roof surface and trims, chimney stacks, window and entrance trims and porch. New York City can record the surface coating, materials of the façade and trim as well as modify any such element described by its construction material.

RECOMMENDATIONS

For an architectural survey the visible materials of the building and its roof are primary questions. Construction technique and materials of the various other elements are secondary questions. Modifying various elements by their individual material is useful.

F. Site and structure: construction elements

ANALYTIC CHART 4F

AR	——	
CA	Roof type	Type du toit (32)
CA	special shape	profils spéciaux (33)
CA	trim eaves	garniture—avant-toit (35)
CA	trim verges	garniture—bordures (37)
CA	special features	particularités (47)
CA	Towers, steeples, domes	Tours, clochers et dômes (39–41)
CA	Dormer type	Type de lucarne (42)
CA	Chimney location	Emplacement de la cheminée (43,44)
CA	Chimney stacks	Des souches (46)
CA	Typical window:	Fenêtre typique:
	location	emplacement (48)
CA	structural opening shape	forme de l'ouverture structurale (49)
CA	trim heads	garniture têtes (50, 55)
CA	trim sides	garniture côtés (51,56)
CA	number of sashes	nombre de châssis (57)
CA	opening mechanism	mécanisme d'ouverture (58)
CA	Special window types	Types particuliers de fenêtres (59)
CA	Special pane arrangements	Disposition particulière des carreaux (60)
CA	Main entrance location	Entrée principale emplacement (61)
CA	structural opening shape	forme de l'ouverture structurale (62)
CA	trim heads	garniture têtes (63,66)
CA	trim sides	garniture côtés (64,67)
CA	Door leaves	Nombre de vantaux (68)
CA	Door panels	Nombre de panneaux (69)
CA	Door special features	Particularités (70)
CA	Mains stairs location	Escalier principal emplacement (71)
CA	direction	direction (72)
FR	Roof type	Type de couverture (1470)
FR	Vault type	Type de couvrement (1480)
FR	Stairways type	Type d'escalier (1500)
IN	——	
IT1	Roof	Copertura
IT1	Vault and attic	Volte e solai
IT1	Stairs	Scale
JP	——	
MX1	Roof shape	Techo de la nave principal
MX1	Number of towers	Número de torres
MA	——	
NYC	Entrance location	(49)
NYC	Door opening	(50)
NYC	Door trim	(51)
NYC	Door type	(52)
NYC	Door panels	(53)
NYC	Porch	(54)
NYC	Window opening	(55)
NYC	Window trim	(56)
NYC	Window type	(57)
NYC	Window panes	(58)
NYC	Roof shape	(59)
NYC	Roof trim	(60)
NYC	Roof features	(61)
NYC	Chimneys	(62)
NYC	Dormer roof	(63)
NYC	Towers under 'building features'	(64)
PL	——	
ZM	——	

DISCUSSION

This topic discusses construction elements such as roof shape, vaulting, stairways, towers, door and windows.

Canada, France, Italy, Mexico and New York City record the roof type or shape. Mexico asks for this only for churches and also counts the number of towers. Canada includes towers with steeples and domes; New York City records towers under Building Features. The vaulting method is described by Italy (*volte e solai*) and France (*type de couvrement*). Italy, France and Canada also mention exterior stairway types and locations. Further specifications are provided by Canada and New York City for the kinds of chimney, dormers, entrance, main door, porch and windows as well as their respective trims.

RECOMMENDATIONS

For an architectural survey, the roof type, vaulting method and stairway are secondary questions. Various other elements and their trims may be included in surveys used for comparative purposes such as those of New York City and Canada.

G. Site and structure: immovable features

ANALYTIC CHART 4G

AR	——	
CA	Wall design and detail	Dessin et détail des murs (31)
FR	Representation	Représentation (1070)
FR	Comments	Précisions (20)
FR	Decoration technique	Technique de décor (1450)
FR	Inscriptions and marks under 'historical commentary'	'Commentaire historique' (60)
IN1	Outstanding features	(6)
IT1	Flooring	Pavimenti
IT1	Exterior decoration	Decorazione esterne
IT1	Interior decoration	Decorazione interne
IT1	Inscriptions, tablets, coats of arms, murals	Iscrizioni, lapidi, stemmi, graffi
IT4	Elements of special interest	Elementi di specifico interesse
JP1	Tablet, inscription and other such items	
MX1	Number of retables	Retablos importantes
MA	——	
NYC	Building features	(64)
NYC	Decorative motifs	(66)
NYC	Significant interior space	(69)
NYC	Architectural sculpture and art	(70)
NYC	Modifiers	(71)
PL3	Interiors under 'description'	'Opis' (13)
ZM	——	

DISCUSSION

Both decorative construction details and attached works of art are discussed as immovable features. Inscriptions, coats of arms, interior and exterior decorations, etc., comprise decorative details. Built-in works of art refer to architectural sculpture, murals, mosaics, etc.

Canada lists decorative features under wall design and detail. New York City includes them as building features or decorative motifs and modifiers. A separate question notes significant interior spaces. Poland includes these under Description. In France inscriptions and marks pertaining to the building campaigns are described under Historical Commentary. Decoration techniques are recorded separately. Japan details tablets and inscriptions and other such items only for National Treasures.

India records inscriptions with sculpture and paintings under Brief History. Italy, in one question, combines inscriptions, tablets, coats of arms and murals. Three questions describe flooring, exterior and interior decoration.

Both the Italian *Catalogo dei beni culturali* and the French *Inventaire général* record on separate forms important works of art. In urban sectors Italy notes *Elementi di specifico interesse* which should be the object of their own forms. France, for artistic works within or on the architectural work but not worthy of an individual form, records the general subject under *Représentation* and specifies the particular event depicted under comments.

New York City records architectural sculpture and art in one question which combines the subject category such as abstract or historical and the method such as mosaic or mural. Mexico counts the number of retables within each church but provides no further description.

RECOMMENDATIONS

Descriptions of immovable features are secondary questions. Inscriptions, tablets, coats of arms, interior and exterior decorations as well as architectural sculpture and art might be recorded but should not be combined with other information such as history. At least two separate questions should be asked; one for decorative details, another for attached art and sculpture. Specifying the general subject and particular event for architectural art and sculpture is useful.

H. Site and structure: movable features

ANALYTIC CHART 4H

AR	——	
CA	Site	Emplacement (10)
FR	Reuse	Remplois (1250)
FR	Displacement	Déplacement (1260)
FR	Museum storage under 'legal status'	'Situation juridique' (1550)
IN	——	
IT1	Furnishings	Arrendamenti
JP	——	
MX	——	
MA3	Movable works of art	Œuvres d'art mobilières
NYC	Moved under 'modifier'	(71)
PL3	Furnishings under 'description'	'Opis' (13)
ZM	Finds	
ZM	Museum object	
ZM	More than one assemblage	

DISCUSSION

Movable features may comprise the structure itself or separate parts of the structure as well as associated furnishings, works of art, finds and specimens. Such features may be movable but *in situ* or they may have been displaced.

Canada, France and New York City record displacement. Since moved buildings are ineligible for national designation by the Canadian Historic Sites and Monuments Board the CIHB notes whether the building is on the original site or has been moved. New York City also records moved structures as well as moved parts. France details displacement to and reuse (*remplois*) from other locations for both parts and totalities.

In a separate question France notes any museum storage for parts which have been moved. Zambia lists the Livingstone Museum object accession number for either specimens or finds from a site. If there is more than one such assemblage this is noted. Finds from a site are classified under Site Type and further described in a non-computerized statement. Furnishings connected with a building are briefly noted by Italy and Poland while Morocco records any movable works of art (*œuvres d'art mobilières*) associated with a monument.

RECOMMENDATIONS

Descriptions of movable features are secondary questions. Various information describing peripatetic structures, parts, or furnishings as well as related works of art, finds and specimens might be recorded. For buildings and parts that have been moved from another location, full citations of the original location may be recorded. For finds and specimens or works of art associated with the structure or site that are in one or various museum collections, all accession numbers might be cross-referenced. This, however, is optional information.

5. Conservation/ restoration/ preservation

ANALYTIC CHART 5

AR12	Conservation condition	Estado de conservación (15,12)
AR1	Adaptability	Grado de adaptabilidad (19)
AR1	Financing	Grado de inversión (20)
CA	Alterations and additions	Modifications et rajouts apparents (77)
FR	Conservation	Conservation (1510)
IN1	Climatic data	(9)
IN1	Conservation chemical notes under 'office files'	(18)
IN1	Structural and chemical conservation ...	(19)
IT14	Conservation status	Stato de conservazione
IT1	Restorations	Restauri
JP23	Requisites for conservation	
MX1	Ruins under 'religious order'	'Orden monastica original'
MX1	Eventual dangers under 'dates of festivals'	'Ferias y fiestas'
MA23	Present state	Etat actuel
MA2	Eventual dangers	Dangers éventuels
MA2	Development perspectives	Perspectives de développement
MA3	Restoration operations	Opérations de restauration
MA3	Restoration perspectives	Perspectives de restauration
MA3	State of conservation	Etat de conservation
MA3	Degree of (conservation) needed	Degré de protection à appliquer
NYC	Alterations to storey	(48)
NYC	Original or unaltered under 'modifier'	(71)
NYC	Vandalized or ruinous under 'modifier'	(71)
PL2	Opinion by conservator	(–)
PL2	Conservator's records	(–)
PL2	Development plan	
PL3	Building works and conservation	Prace budowlane i konserwatorskie (18)
PL3	State of preservation	Stan zachowania (19)
PL3	Type and scope of conservation measures	Najpilniejsze postulaty konserwatorskie (20)
ZM	Present condition under 'other information'	

DISCUSSION

Since problems of meaning occur with the terms 'conservation, restoration and preservation' the three are grouped together here and generally mean the professional practices of rescue and physical maintenance for a site or structure. This category discusses: the present condition or actual state of conservation; past technical works previously undertaken; and perspectives as well as necessary work for future conservation.

Most systems describe the present condition of the site or structure. Canada, New York City, Zambia and France record only the present condition. Any apparent alterations or additions to the original fabric are noted by Canada. New York City modifies elements which may be missing or altered, vandalized or ruined. Zambia may comment upon the present condition of the site under Other Information. France, under Conservation, includes the possibilities of ruins, bad state (mauvais état), menaced (menacé) and restored. If the entry is in good condition the question is not answered.

For churches Mexico includes ruins under Religious Order. Argentina asks about conservation condition for both monuments and sites. For both sites and districts, Japan combines the present condition with needed work in one question, Requisites for Conservation.

Poland, Morocco and Italy specify the condition of separate parts of the building. Poland describes the condition of the foundations, walls, vaults, floors, rafters, roofing, furnishings and services. Morocco, for individual monuments, details the state of conservation in a multiple-choice grid. This notes as satisfactory, mediocre or bad the condition of the total work, parts, roof, interior, ceiling and terraces. Any humidity or condensation is also mentioned.

For architecture Italy also codes in a grid format the conservation status (stato de conservazione) on a six-point scale for walls, roof, attic, vaults and ceiling, subterranean structure, flooring, decoration, surfaces, plaster and fixtures. The six possibilities are excellent (ottimo), good (buono), mediocre (mediocre), bad (cattivo), very bad (pessimo), and ruined (rudere). Also the date of conservation inspection is noted. Any specific damage and its cause are mentioned as observations. A similar grid, but less elaborate and undated, describes the conservation status of each parcel in an Urban Sector.

Only India, Italy and Poland describe previous conservation or restoration work. India records outstanding structural and chemical conservation 'so far carried out'. Additional conservation notes may be cross-referenced in the question Office Files. Italy briefly lists both old and more recent restorations by date and type. Poland, in the question Building Works and Conservation, describes earlier conservation practices and references available documentation for inventoried buildings. Their Cover Sheet for Historic Cities and Towns cross-references the date and number of the conservator's records.

For future conservation several systems record either perspectives or practices which may include dangers, technical information or needed work. Japan, Morocco and Poland mention the level of need. Japan combines work to be performed with actual condition in the one question, Requisites for Conservation. Poland asks about conservation measures urgently needed. Morocco, for monuments, describes the degree of conservation necessary (total or partial) or the need for reconstruction. Additional questions Perspectives de Restauration and Opérations de Restauration record future and current practices.

Mexico, India and Morocco all include specific information useful for planning future conservation. Mexican fiestas are the pretext for the most common unauthorized alterations to churches so these dates are recorded to signal potential maintenance problems. India collects climatic data such as temperature and rainfall to help identify likely geographic areas for particular difficulties and solutions. Morocco, for Sites, suggests eventual dangers.

In addition Poland, Argentina and Morocco discuss development possibilities. Here the Development Plan for Historic Cities and Towns is referenced by Poland. For monuments Argentina mentions possible adaptability (grado de adaptabilidad) as well as financing (grado de inversión). Morocco also notes development opportunities for sites.

RECOMMENDATIONS

The general present condition of the total site or structure is a primary question. This pin-points both the obvious ruins and urgently menaced entries. The condition of specific parts is a secondary question and for professional recording only. Grid formats that provide standard levels of condition and specify the separate building parts are useful. Specific condition information should be dated and kept current.

Past conservation or restoration work previously completed is an optional question. Only brief references should be made by the survey to other complete dossiers that contain precise information. References should cite, in chronological sequence, the date, type or work and official record number and identify where the record is stored.

Future conservation or preservation information is a secondary question. Information may record the level needed or describe the particular work. Data may preview eventual dangers as well as suggest future developments, including adaptability, and necessary financing.

6. Documentation/reference

A. Published bibliography

ANALYTIC CHART 6A

AR12	Bibliography	Bibliografía (22,14)
CA	Sources under 'observations'	'Observations' (–)
FR	Text microfiche	N° microfiche texte (5)
FR	Continuation	Mise à jour de la microfiche (80)
IN1	Published references	(7)
IT12	Bibliography	Bibliografica
JP	——	
MX	——	
MA23	Basic bibliography	Bibliographie de base
NYC	——	
PL3	Literature references	Bibliografia (22)
ZM	Publications	

DISCUSSION

The Documentation/Reference Category is divided into five topics. The first, Published Bibliography, discusses publication references. The other four topics generally cover non-published supportive documentation.

Canada cites any sources used to record the entry under the question called Observations but does not computerize this information. France stores full bibliographic references in text on microfiche. The appropriate microfiche numbers are cross-referenced on the *bordereau architecture*. If additional microfiches are used the continuation numbers are noted (*mise à jour de la microfiche*). Argentina records bibliography divided into books, publications and other. India includes published references such as Imperial and District Gazettes and local manuals.

Italy, under the question *Bibliografica*, cites each publication in chronological order and notes the author, title, place of publication, year, pages, and plates. Morocco lists basic bibliography. Poland, for architecture, includes a question called Literature References. Zambia records publications in full citations but only computerizes the fact that some publication exists.

RECOMMENDATIONS

Complete bibliography is an optional question. Such references must be exhaustive and current to be useful. Therefore, a comprehensive bibliography necessitates a separate documentation method utilizing microfiches or specialized computer programs. If separate bibliographies exist, cross-references should be made on the recording form to the relevant entry such as a text microfiche number.

Restricted bibliography is a secondary question. Citations should follow a standard format. Zambia's recording of full citations, but computerizing only the fact that some publication exists, is worth noting.

B. Files and reports

ANALYTIC CHART 6B

AR	——	
CA	Archaeological site	Site archéologique (83)
CA	Reference	Référence (84)
FR	Dossier under 'documentation reference'	'Documentation référence' (5)
IN1	Office files	(18)
IT1	Technical reports	Realzioni techniche
JP	——	
MX2	Office file number	Número en clave
MA23	Studies and reports	Etudes et rapports
NYC	Research resources	(72)
PL1	*List of Historic Monuments*	
PL1	*Catalogue of Ancient Objects*	
PL2	Archaeological data	
PL2	Town-planning survey	
PL2	File No.	(–)
PL2	Historical and town-planning surveys	(–)
ZM	Office file number	
ZM	Additional files	
ZM	Excavations	

DISCUSSION

Within this topic office files and other reports are discussed. France, Mexico and Zambia make general references to office files; Canada and India specify particular information.

France codes whether an office dossier has been used to complete the *bordereau architecture*. Mexico, for monuments and places of natural beauty, computerizes the relevant office file number (*número en clave*) but it is not asked for on the form. Zambia records the office file number for either the National Monuments Commission or the Livingstone Museum. However, only one file number is computerized together with the fact that others may exist. File numbers are not necessarily provided for sites that have been published.

India, within the question Office Files, mentions inspection, conservation, administrative, horticultural and epigraphic notes held within the Circle Office. Canada, in the question Reference, codes the existence of other CIHB reports, files and Phase II information on building interiors.

Individual studies and reports may also be identified. Canada notes the existence of information held by the archaeology division under the question Archaeological Site; the information itself is not identified. Archaeological excavations connected with the site are recorded by Zambia in full citations but only the fact that such excavations have been made is computerized. Poland also references archaeological data on the Cover Sheet of the Historic Cities and Towns Inventory. In addition, historical and town-planning surveys are identified.

New York City points out the existence of the entry in other surveys such as the national HABS (Historic American Building Survey) in the question Research Resources. Poland mentions if the entry is in the *List of Historic Monuments* or the *Catalogue of Ancient Objects*. Morocco records unspecified Studies and Reports for both monuments and sites. For architecture Italy references Technical Reports held in the office.

RECOMMENDATIONS

Files and reports is a secondary question. References to office files may record either the fact that some files exist (France, Mexico, or Zambia) or may specify the kind of information contained within the file (India, Canada). File numbers should be cross-referenced. The files themselves remain separate from the survey form.

Reports and studies in addition to office files may be indicated. These may either be unspecified (Morocco) or specified (New York City).

Generally these reports also remain separate from the survey; they may be either held by the survey or known to the survey. Full citations should be made for author, title, place of publication, and date.

C. Maps, plans and drawings

ANALYTIC CHART 6C

AR12	Plans—ensemble, floors, details, cross-sections, views, perspectives	Planos—conjunto, plantas, detalles, cortes, vistas, perspectivas (23,15)
AR12	(Microfiches)	
CA	Dominion land survey maps	Arpentage des terres fédérales (–)
CA	Plans and drawings under 'reference'	'Référence' (84)
FR	Photogrammetry and measured drawings under 'documentation reference'	'Documentation référence' (5)
FR	Photo microfiches	N° de microfiche photo (5)
IN1	Drawings	(23)
IT12	Extracts from cadastral maps	Estratto mappa catastale
IT1	Maps	Mappa
IT1	Plans and drawings	Disengi e rilievi
IT1	Engravings	Stampe
IT2	Profiles	Profili
IT2	Assembled plans	Planimetrie
JP1	Number of drawing	
JP2	(Count) of sheets of maps, drawings, prints	
JP3	(Map and drawing)	
MX1	Plans, if possible	Planos si es posible
MA23	Plans and maps	Plans et cartes
NYC	——	
PL2	(Maps)	
PL3	Plan, situation ·	Plan sytuacyjny, rzuty (11)
ZM	——	

DISCUSSION

The topic, Maps, Plans and Drawings, discusses maps that locate the entry within a larger context as well as plans and drawings that visually detail the entry itself. (For a discussion of maps used for Cartographic Co-ordinates see p. 103.) Some systems (Canada, France) merely reference the existence of this information; others (Argentina, India, Italy, Japan, Morocco and Poland) attach or enclose copies of the documentation with the form. In addition, scales of measurement as well as particular views or details may be specified.

Canada identifies the relevant Dominion Land Survey map but this information is not computerized. Japan, for Historic Sites, attaches copies of survey maps to the Ledger. The actual count of the map sheets is cross-referenced in a question. For Districts, copies of the survey maps are attached but no reference is made on the form.

Morocco, for both Sites and Monuments, references maps and plans in one question. Copies may be attached on the reverse of the forms.

Poland includes maps within the Historic Cities file but no reference is made on the Cover Sheet. For buildings, Poland attaches a map to the front of the Inventory Sheet. This depicts location utilizing a set scale of 1:25,000 for towns or 1:250 or 1:500 for rural structures.

All Italian documentation is specified as being enclosed (*allegati*) or not. Extracts copied from the relevant cadastral maps are always enclosed and referenced by number on the forms. Other maps are identified as either enclosed or not.

Mexico requests plans from volunteer recorders if available, but does not record their existence. Canada codes the existence of files containing plans and sketches. France notes on the *bordereau architecture* whether photogrammetric or measured drawings exist. Such documentation is stored on microfiches.

Argentina, India, Japan and Morocco attach plans or drawings to the forms. Argentina subdivides plans into various types—of the ensemble, floors, details, cross-sections, views and perspectives. When none exist they are made specially. Copies are attached to the form. Documentation will eventually be stored on microfiche. Japan, for National Treasures and Historic Sites, attaches drawings (and for Sites, prints as well) to the Ledger and counts the number of sheets in a separate question; for Districts, Japan attaches drawings but does not reference them on the form. Morocco records plans (with maps) and may attach copies on the reverse of the form. India references drawings held in the Circle Office and pastes selected sketches on attached sheets for the Record.

Both Poland and Italy include plans with a set scale. Poland attaches building plans with a scale of 1:100, 1:200 or 1:400 as well as basic measurements and north indicated. Italy, for architecture and urban sectors, encloses plans (*rilievi*). For buildings, the scale is 1:100 or 1:50; for urban sectors, 1:200. For buildings there is always a floor plan showing construction phases as well as a view of the type of structure plus perspectives or sections. Additional plans and drawings, either attached or located elsewhere, are identified. Engravings are noted. For urban

sectors profiles and assembled plans are also included.

RECOMMENDATIONS

Maps, plans and drawings is a secondary question. References may record either the general fact that some information exists (Morocco and Canada) or may specify the kind of information that exists (France, Argentina). Particular information may be requested (Mexico, Poland, Italy).

Mexico's appeal to volunteer recorders for available plans is worth noting. Italy and Poland specify the types of plans to be professionally prepared especially for the survey. France notes the existence of professional photogrammetric or measured drawings.

Maps, plans and drawings may be separate from the survey form and indicated on it. They may be held by the survey or be known to the survey and located elsewhere. All should be fully referenced including location for those not held. In addition maps, plans and drawings may be attached to or enclosed within the form itself. These attachments should be fully labelled by name and number and source. They should be fully identified on the form as well. Copies only, of course, and not original documentation should be attached to the form.

D. Photographs

ANALYTIC CHART 6D

AR12	Photographs—interior, exterior, aerial	Fototografías—interiores, exteriores, aéreas (24,16)
AR12	(Microfiches)	
CA	Total photos	Nombre total de photos (–)
CA	Film-roll number	N° de la bobine de film (–)
CA	Photographer's name	Photographe (–)
CA	Historical photos and slides under 'reference'	'Référence' (84)
FR	Photo microfiches	N° microfiche photo (5)
FR	Continuation	Mise à jour de la microfiche (80)
IN1	Photographs	(22)
IT12	Photographs	Fotografie
IT2	Air photos	Fotografie aerie
IT2	Photos of historic plans	Fotografi di pianta storiche
JP1	Number of photograph	
JP2	(Total) sheets of photos	
JP2	No. of photograph ledger	
MX1	Photographs	Fotografías
MA23	Photographs, slides, films	Photographies, diapositives, films
NYC	Film-roll number	(11)
NYC	First and last shot	(12–13)
NYC	Additional film rolls under 'research resources'	(72)
PL3	Photographs, situation and plan	Zdjecia, …(11)
PL3	Illustrative sources and photographs	Zródla ikonograficzne i fotografie (23)
ZM	——	

DISCUSSION

France utilizes professional photographic documentation which is stored on microfiche. Reference is made on the *bordereau architecture* to the appropriate photo microfiche. If additional microfiches are used, the continuation number is noted (*mise à jour de la microfiche*). Argentina plans to use microfiches. In addition, on the forms Argentina subdivides photo types into interior, exterior and aerial. If no photos exist, they are taken and copies are attached to the form.

Mexico requests photos; India, Italy, Japan, Morocco and Poland record photos and attach them to the survey forms. Mexico solicits photos, if available, from volunteer recorders, but does not record their existence. India notes photos held in the Circle Office and attaches selected examples to the Record. Morocco mentions photos, slides and films for both monuments and sites. Copies of photos are attached to the reverse of the forms.

Japan attaches photos to each Ledger. For both National Treasures and Historic Sites, the photo sheets are counted; for Sites, the Photo Ledger is identified as well. No reference is made for Preservation District photos on that Ledger form, however.

Poland includes contemporary photos of town-planning features in the Historic Cities file as well as photos of historic maps. However, no reference is made on the Cover Sheet to the photos within. For buildings, Poland attaches at least one 6 × 9 black-and-white photograph to the front of the inventory sheet. Photos held in-house or by the system, are identified by photographer, date, name of building and storage place. Within a separate question, Illustrative Sources and Photographs, the storage place and negative number for non-held photographs are identified.

Italy folds or encloses photographs in form. Non-held photographs are also identified. Both are referenced by negative number, date and source. For Urban Sectors aerial photos and photos of historic plans are also included.

Neither Canada nor New York City attach photographs to the recording form but contact prints are attached to a separate photo card for office use. Both photograph every entry in the inventory on black-and-white 35 mm film. Film rolls are identified. Canada records the name of the photographer and counts the number of shots taken. New York City records the number of the first and last shot taken as well as in a separate question any additional rolls and shots. For New York all photographic information is computerized.

Italy and Poland both include photographic reproductions of historic plans in their documentation for Urban Sectors or Historic Cities and Towns. For each entry, Canada codes the existence of slides or any historic photographs stored in office files. Morocco also references slides and films in addition to photographs.

Argentina references aerial photographs. Italy encloses aerial photos for Urban Sectors. Mexico planned to interpret aerial photos to compensate for gaps in volunteer recording, but no mention of this is made on the forms.

RECOMMENDATIONS

New photographs specially taken for the survey, and their citation, are primary information. Photographer, date, subject, film roll and negative shots as well as place of storage must be identified.

References to other photographs are secondary information. These may be either held by the survey or physically located elsewhere. All should be fully identified by photographer, date, subject, film roll and negative number. For photographs in other collections the place of storage should always be cited.

Actual photographs, either new or old, may remain separate from the survey form and only be indicated on the form. They may be attached or enclosed with the form itself. Any attachments should be fully labelled and also identified on the form.

The sub-division of photographic documentation by the type such as interior, exterior, aerial, historical, slides, etc. is useful. Mexico's appeal to volunteer recorders to send photographs, if available, can be contrasted with the rigours of methodically photographing every entry in a standard fashion. Both approaches are valid and depend on budget and need.

For large collections of photographic documentation, microfiche provides an economic means for both duplication and storage. Cross-references should always be made on the recording form to the relevant microfiche number.

E. Other information

ANALYTIC CHART 6E

AR	——	
CA	Observations	Observations (–)
FR	——	
IN12	Remarks	(24,9)
IT12	Archives	Archivi
IT12	Other documents	Documenti vari
IT12	Other forms	Alte schede
IT12	Subgroup number	N°
IT2	Extract from Centro Storico	Straclio di parte de Centro Storico
IT2	Iconography	Iconografici
IT2	Inserts	Repertorio relativo
IT3	Documents	Documenti
JP2	Remarks	
JP2	No. of reports on	
JP3	Other items of reference	
MX1	(Oldest document in parish archives)	Que época existen documentos
MA23	Other archives	Autres archives
MA23	Cf. number	Cf. numéro
MA2	Observations	Observations
NYC	——	
PL1	Provided with inventory sheet	
PL2	Table of contents	
PL23	Remarks	Uwagi rózne (24)
PL3	Archival materials	Akta archiwalne ... (21)
ZM	Other information	

DISCUSSION

Other information includes archival sources and references to miscellaneous reports. Questions such as Observations and Remarks provide for contingencies. Other forms within the same system may be cross-referenced.

Italy (*archivi*), Morocco (*autres archives*) and Poland (archival materials) generally refer to archival material. Within the citation Poland lists the type of information, place of storage and call marks. Mexico for religious architecture asks for the period of the oldest document within each parish archive but computerizes the actual date.

Italy references other documents (*documentari vari*) and encloses copies within the forms. For Urban Sectors Italy also includes documentation on *iconografici* and on an extract from the relevant Historical Centre form (*straclio di parte de Centro Storico*). On the Historic Research insert for the Urban Sector, separate documentation for each parcel is cited.

Poland includes a table of contents on the Historic Cities and Towns Cover Sheet. Japan, for Historic Sites, identifies (unspecified) reports or other items of reference.

Canada, Japan, Morocco and Zambia include contingency questions. Such terms as 'remarks', 'observations' or 'other information' provide a specific place on the forms to record additional information. For example, Canada includes in Observations all pertinent data not coded on the form such as special details, simple sketches and sources used in recording.

Italy, Poland and Morocco cross-reference the various other forms included within their individual systems. Within Italy's *Catalogo dei beni culturali* other forms are cross-referenced in a standard question (*altre schede*). The Urban Sector form also separately references each of the inserts for Historical Research and Present Condition. A separate subgroup number distinguishes related forms such as each chapel of a church. For Urban Sectors this identifies the particular sector within the larger historic centre.

Morocco cross-references Sites and Monuments and vice versa by giving their related type-order numbers. Poland, on the brief Address Form notes whether the entry has been provided with the more complete Inventory Sheet. On the building Inventory Sheet itself cross-references to other forms within the Polish system are included in the question called Remarks.

RECOMMENDATIONS

Additional References is a secondary question used to identify documentation not mentioned elsewhere on the form. This information may be held by the survey or known to the survey and physically located elsewhere. In addition, it may remain separate from the forms where it is identified or it may be attached, or included with, the forms. Citation information should be complete and state the type of information, date, location of the source, and any call marks.

Contingencies is a primary question. Since no system can possibly deal with all possibilities such terms as 'remarks' or 'observations' provide a set place on the form to record the 'unknown whatevers' which may occur.

Cross-references to other relevant forms are a primary question. This may be to a subgroup within the same category of form or to other categories within the same system. Forms should be identified by type and number.

7. Systematization

A. Recording record

AR	——	
CA	Date of survey	Date de l'enquête (79)
CA	Team number	N° de l'équipe (–)
CA	Name of photographer	Photographe (–)
CA	Name of recorder	Enquêteur (–)
CA	(Certainty code)	(–)
FR	Dossier under 'documentation reference'	'Documentation reference' (5)
IN1	Approach	(5)
IN1	Inspection notes under 'office files'	(18)
IN1	Superintendent's signature and date	(25)
IT1234	Ministry	Ministerio
IT1234	Department (and code)	Soprintendenza
IT12	Compiler	Compilatore
IT12	Date	Data
IT12	Approved by	Visto del soprintendente
IT12	Revisions	Revisioni
JP	——	
MX	——	
MA23	Drafted by and date	Rédigée par le
MA23	Checked by and date	Contrôlée par le
MA23	Revised by and date	Révisée par le
MA23	Visited by	Visité par
MA23	Date	Date
MA23	Number of dossier	N° du dossier
NYC	Inspection date under 'date of change'	(27)
PL3	Photographer's name and date under 'photographs …'	(11)
PL3	Prepared by and date	Wypelnil (25)
PL3	Checked by and date	Sprawdzil (26)
ZM	Source/informant	
ZM	Unconfirmed under 'status'	

DISCUSSION

The recording record states who (or what) provided the record and when. Either the actual source for the entry record or the person(s) who collected the information and the date are identified. In addition, it may state who checked the entry or revised it, and may give an official signature of approval. Some systems also record actual site inspection.

B. Systematics

ANALYTIC CHART 7B

AR12	Inventory number	Número de inventario (1,1)
CA	Geocode	Géocode (–)
FR	Machine number	N° machine (1000)
IN2	Serial no.	(1)
IT1234	Type of dossier	Typo di dossier
IT1234	Catalogue general number	Numero di catalogo generale
IT1234	International catalogue number	Numero di catalogo internazionale
JP3	Selection number	
MX	——	
MA1	Type-order number	Type-n° d'ordre
MA1	Computer line number	C.c.
MA23	(Type-order) number	N°
NYC	Geocode	(–)
NYC	Batch	(–)
NYC	Record no.	(–)
PL13	(Alpha-colour codes)	
PL3	Number	Nr (–)
ZM	——	

DISCUSSION

Systematics discusses those questions within each system which organize information. Some of these questions are answered in serial numbers (assigned in simple sequence); other answers are coded to represent various types of information. Used by both manual and computer systems, entry numbers provide unique identification. Other numbers determine office codes or are used for computer purposes such as batch or line numbers.

Argentina will use a coded inventory number on each form. France assigns a machine number for each entry. Poland, on the building Inventory Sheet, includes a place for an eventual computer number. Across the top of both this and the Address Form an alpha-colour code identifies style, type and ownership for office use.

On Zambian print-out a computer line number appears. However, this is not a main entry number. Zambia deliberately rejected computer entry by numeric code, choosing instead entry by site name.

India, on its brief List, gives a sequential serial number to every entry within each state. No number is provided on the complete record. Japan, for Preservation Districts, assigns a sequential selection number to each entry. This number is repeated on every page of the Ledger format for that particular district. No number distinguishes Treasures or Sites.

Morocco, Italy, Canada and New York City all use coded numbers to identify each entry within their systems. On all forms Morocco assigns a six-digit type-order number. This determines, in the first two digits, one of sixty-five use-types and in the additional four digits the numeric sequence of the particular entry within that type. On the computerized format for the *Liste Générale,* each line of entry repeats the type-order number and is identified with a unique line number (c.c.).

Italy combines an alpha code with a ten-digit *numero di catalogo generale* to provide the unique identifier. The pre-printed alphabetic prefix distinguishes the category of form. For example, A is for *Architettura,* SU for *Sectore Urbano.* The general catalogue number is assigned at the Istituto Centrale. The first two digits give the region; the last eight digits establish the numeric sequence within the region. In addition, space is provided prefaced with ITA for a future international catalogue number.

Canada and New York City both use a geocode for unique entry identification. For urban Canada, fifteen digits numerically code province, city and street address. For rural areas, province, map number and location number on the map make up the geocode. The thirteen-digit New York City geocode combines borough, block, lot and parcel codes. This is repeated seven times to distinguish the beginning of each new line of computer entry. The computer line number (record No.) is pre-printed. The batch number for computer punching is assigned sequentially; 1000 forms within the same borough comprise a batch.

RECOMMENDATIONS

The entry number is a primary question. However, it should only be assigned by professional staff within the main office. This provides terse unique identification for each entry within the system around which all other information can be organized. It should be repeated on all separate documentation relevant to the entry as well, on front and back of all forms.

Sequential entry numbers determine how many entries exist within the system. The highest number corresponds to the total number of entries. Coded entry numbers compact a great deal of information into a few digits.

Other information, as for office codes and computer batches, are secondary questions. Alpha-colour codes for office use help provide quick identification for manual filing. For computerized systems the repetition of the identification number on each line helps to organize all data for each entry. Batch numbers organize large groups of forms.

Planning worksheet

1. Purpose and objectives	
2. Criteria	A. Scope or coverage B. Selection C. Legal
3. Users and products	Components
4. Existing resources	A. Staff B. Volunteers C. Outside assistance
5. Method	A. Computerization B. Standardization
6. Costs and time	

(For general instructions see Part One—Methodology)

Question Typology

PRIMARY INFORMATION SECONDARY INFORMATION OPTIONAL INFORMATION

1 IDENTIFICATION/LOCATION

OTHER

	PRIMARY INFORMATION	SECONDARY INFORMATION	OPTIONAL INFORMATION
1A NAME	Present name	Past or alternative name(s) Modifier	
1B TYPOLOGY, USE	Type	Present or actual use(s) Past or original use(s) Future or possible use(s)	
1C ADDRESS	Geographic-administrative address Specific address	Alternative names for the locality Alternative address Position or directions Approach Specifics	
1D COORDINATES, PROPERTY REGISTRATION		Cartographic coordinates .... Attach map sheet Legal registration	
1E OWNERSHIP		Ownership type Present owner's name Tenant or responsible office Original owner	

2 SIGNIFICANCE/DESIGNATION

	PRIMARY INFORMATION	SECONDARY INFORMATION	OPTIONAL INFORMATION
2A IMPORTANCE	Level of importance		
2B OFFICIAL DESIGNATION AND OTHER LEGALITIES	Level of protection and designation .... Update Name, number and date .... Attach copy of text Legal criteria Announcement Future designation		

3 DATE HISTORY

	PRIMARY INFORMATION	SECONDARY INFORMATION	OPTIONAL INFORMATION
3A DATE	Period and/or years Demolition or destruction .... Update Accuracy/certainty	Commencement and completions Changes	
3B HISTORICAL COMMENTARY		Construction campaigns or building history Historical events Legends and traditions	
3C AUTHORSHIP		Name(s) and professional roles Accuracy/certainty	

4 DESCRIPTION

	PRIMARY INFORMATION	SECONDARY INFORMATION	OPTIONAL INFORMATION
4A AREA		Quantification Urbanistic relationships	
SETTING		Situation, placement, ambience Features Personnel	
SITE/ STRUCTURE			
4B MAGNITUDE		Magnitude :Dimensions :Plan type :Massing, volume	
4C GEN. DESC.		General description .... Not recommended	
4D STYLE		Styles .... Not for volunteers	

4E MATERIALS, TECHNIQUES	Visible materials of total structure	. . . .	. . . . For architecture
	Materials of specific parts		
	Construction technique		
4F CONSTRUCTION ELEMENTS	Construction elements	Roof	
		Vaulting	
		Stairways	
		Other	
4G IMMOVABLE FEATURES	Immovable features	Decorative details	
		Art and sculpture	
		Representation	
4H MOVABLE FEATURES	Movable features	Structure, parts	
		Other location	
		Furnishings and works of art	
		Finds, specimens	
		Accession numbers	

5 CONSERVATION/RESTORATION/PRESERVATION

5A PRESENT CONDITION	General condition of site or structure		
	Actual condition of specific parts · · · · : : · . · . ·	· . · . · . · . Not for volunteers	
		. . . . Update	
5A PAST WORK	Citation references to: . . Separate files		
5A FUTURE PERSPECTIVES	Necessary level		
	Specific work		
	Dangers		
	Development		
	Adaptability		
	Financing		

6 DOCUMENTATION/REFERENCE

6A PUBLISHED BIBLIOGRAPHY	Cross-reference to: . . . Comprehensive bibliography		
	Text microfiche		
	Restricted bibliography		
	Complete citation		
6B FILES AND REPORTS	Cross-reference to: . . Separate office files		
	Citation reference to: . . Separate studies and reports		
	Specified or unspecified		
6C MAPS, PLANS, DRAWINGS	Citation reference to: . . Separate maps . . . . Attach copy		
	plans, drawings		
	Specified or unspecified		
	Indicated, held or attached		
	Microfiche		
6D PHOTOGRAPHS	New photographs	. . . . Attach copy	
	Complete citation		
	Citation reference to: . . Separate photographs		
	Specified or unspecified		
	Indicated, held, attached		
	Cross-reference to: . . . Photo microfiche		
6E OTHER INFORMATION	Citation reference to: . . Separate archives		
	Contingencies	. . Miscellaneous . . . . Attach Copy	
	Remarks or observations		
	Other forms		Attach copy

7 SYSTEMATIZATION

7A RECORDING RECORD	Date and source-compiler for form	Form checked, revised, approved	
		Citation reference to: . . Separate site inspection file	
	Certainty		
		Name of inspector	
7B SYSTEMATICS	Identification number	. . . .	. . . . Not for volunteers
		Other numbers	

System comparison chart

Argentina (AR)
Sistema Automadizado de Inventario y
Registro de Monumentos y Sitios

Canada (CA)
Canadian Inventory of Historic Building

France (FR)
Inventaire Général des Monuments et
des Richesses Artistiques de la France

India (IN)
Record of Protected Monuments and Sites

Italy (IT)
Catalogo dei Beni Culturali

Japan (JP)
Ledger of Designated Cultural Property

Mexico (MX)
Catalogación Sistema Culhuacán

Morocco (MA)
Inventaire National du Patrimoine
Culturel

New York City (NYC)
Urban Cultural Resources Survey

Poland (PL)
System of Inventorying Historical
Monuments

Zambia (ZM)
Zambia National Site Index

Reproductions
of original forms

Parks Parcs
Canada Canada

NATIONAL HISTORIC PARKS AND SITES BRANCH _ **DIRECTION DES LIEUX ET DES PARCS HISTORIQUES NATIONAUX**
CANADIAN INVENTORY OF HISTORIC BUILDING **L'INVENTAIRE DES BÂTIMENTS HISTORIQUES DU CANADA**

Province / Territory - *Province / Territoire*

Total No. of Photos Taken
Nombre total de photos

Film Roll No.
N° de la bobine de film

Town - *Ville*

Team No. - *N° de l'équipe*

County - *Comté*

District - *District*

Township - *Canton*

Street - *Rue*

Map No. - *N° de la carte*

Building No. - *N° du bâtiment*

Building No. on Map - *N° du bâtiment sur la carte*

Concession No. - *N° de concession*

Lot No. - *N° de lot*

Dominion Land Survey
Arpentage des terres fédérales

Present Owner - *Propriétaire actuel*

Address of Owner - *Adresse du propriétaire*

Tenant - *Locataire*

Original Owner or Tenant - *Propriétaire ou locataire d'origine*

Building Name - *Nom du bâtiment*

Recorder - *Enquêteur*

Photographer - *Photographe*

Province Geocode - *Géocode*

▶ Attach Photos Below
Annexer les photos ci-dessous

Year(s) of Construction
Année(s) de construction

Known
Données connues **K**

Estimated
Données estimatives **E** **A** **R**

Year of Demolition
Année de démolition

Known
Données connues **K**

Estimated
Données estimatives **E** **A** **R**

Province / Territory
Province / Territoire

Town
Ville

County or District
Comté ou district

Township
Canton

Street
Rue

Building No.
N° du bâtiment

Map No.
N° de la carte

Building No. on Map
N° du bâtiment sur la carte

Concession No. and Lot No.
N° de concession et N° de lot

Dominion Land Survey
Arpentage des terres fédérales

Date of Survey
Date de l'enquête

DAY
JOUR

MONTH
MOIS

YEAR
ANNÉE

PC 824 (12-79)

145

CA: Original form.

OBSERVATIONS:

Present Owner
Propriétaire actuel

Address of Owner
Adresse du propriétaire

Observations - *Observations*

Tenant
Locataire

Original Owner or Tenant
Propriétaire ou locataire d'origine

Building Name
Nom du bâtiment

Architect
Architecte

Major Contractor or Builder
Entrepreneur principal ou constructeur

Engineer
Ingénieur

| Negatives Négatifs | ☐ | Team No. N° de l'équipe | | |

PC 824 (12-79)

1 YEAR(S) OF CONSTRUCTION / ANNÉE(S) DE CONSTRUCTION

Known Données connues **K** Estimated Données estimatives **E**

OFFICE USE ONLY
À L'USAGE DU BUREAU SEULEMENT

A **R**

2 YEAR OF DEMOLITION / ANNÉE DE DÉMOLITION

Known Données connues **K** Estimated Données estimatives **E**

OFFICE USE ONLY — À L'USAGE DU BUREAU SEULEMENT

A **R**

3 ARCHITECT / ARCHITECTE

A — Code
B — Code
C — Code

4 MAJOR CONTRACTOR OR BUILDER / ENTREPRENEUR PRINCIPAL OU CONSTRUCTEUR

A — Code
B — Code
C — Code

5 ENGINEER / INGÉNIEUR

A — Code
B — Code
C — Code

6 PRESENT USE / USAGE ACTUEL

Primary Use / Usage principal

Secondary Use / Usage secondaire

7 ORIGINAL USE / USAGE INITIAL

Unknown / Inconnu   Same / Même

Primary Use / Usage principal

Secondary Use / Usage secondaire

8 ASSOCIATED OR OTHER USES / USAGES APPARENTÉS OU AUTRES

9 STATE / ÉTAT

Not Applicable / Non applicable   Abandoned / Abandonné   Vacant / Inhabité   Occupied / Habité

10 SITE / EMPLACEMENT

Unknown / Inconnu   Original / Initial   Moved / Déplacé   Other / Autre

PC 824 (12-79)

147

11

12

13

14

15

16

17

18

19

20

21

22

23

24

25

26

27

28

1	2	3	4
5	6	7	8
9	10		

29

30

31

1	2	3	4
5	6	7	8
9	10	11	12
13	14	15	16
17	18	19	20
21	22	23	24
25	26	27	28
29	30	31	32
33	34	35	36
37			

32

33

1	2	3	4
5	6	7	8
9	10		

34

35

1	2	3	4
5	6	7	8
9	10	11	12
13	14	15	16

36

37

1	2	3	4
5	6	7	8
9	10	11	12
13	14	15	16
17	18		

38

39

| 1 | 2 | 3 | 4 |
| 5 | 6 | | |

40

1	2	3	4
5	6	7	8
9	10		

41

1	2	3	4
5	6	7	8
9	10		

42

1	2	3	4
5	6	7	8
9	10	11	12
13	14	15	16
17	18	19	20
21	22	23	

43

1	2	3	4
5	6	7	8
9	10		

44

1	2	3	4
5	6	7	8
9	10		

45

1	2	3	4
5	6	7	8
9			

46

| 1 | 2 | 3 | 4 |
| 5 | 6 | 7 | 8 |

47

1	2	3	4
5	6	7	8
9	10	11	12
13			

48

49

50

1	2	3	4
5	6	7	8
9	10	11	12
13	14	15	16
17	18	19	20
21	22	23	24
25	26		

51

1	2	3	4
5	6	7	8
9	10	11	12
13			

52

53

54

55

1	2	3	4
5	6	7	8
9	10	11	

56

1	2	3	4
5	6	7	8
9	10	11	12

57

58

59

1	2	3	4
5	6	7	8
9	10	11	12
13	14	15	16
17	18	19	20
21	22	23	24

60

1	2	3	4
5	6	7	8
9	10	11	12
13	14	15	16
17	18	19	20
21	22	23	24
25			

61

62

63

1	2	3	4
5	6	7	8
9	10	11	12
13	14	15	16
17	18	19	20
21	22	23	24
25	26		

64

1	2	3	4
5	6	7	8
9	10	11	12
13			

65

66

1	2	3	4
5	6	7	8
9	10	11	

67

1	2	3	4
5	6	7	8
9	10	11	12

68

69

70

1	2	3	4
5	6	7	8
9	10	11	

71

72

73

74

1	2	3	4
5	6	7	8
9	10	11	12
13	14		

75

76

77

1	2	3	4
5	6	7	8
9	10	11	12
13	14		

78

| 1 | 2 | 3 | 4 |
| 5 | | | |

79

80

81

82

83

84

| A | D | G | H |
| S | I | P | |

PC 824 (12-79)

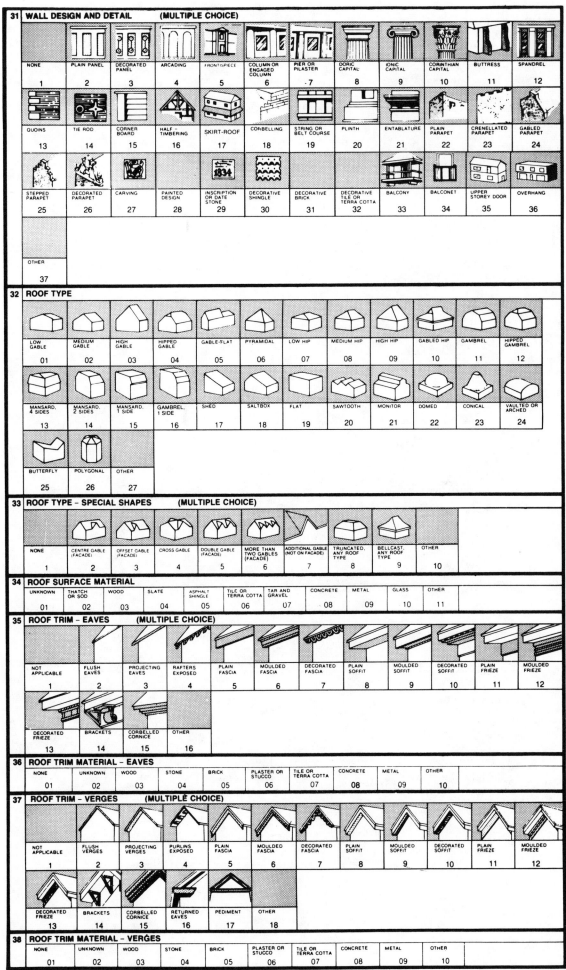

31 WALL DESIGN AND DETAIL (MULTIPLE CHOICE)

NONE 1	PLAIN PANEL 2	DECORATED PANEL 3	ARCADING 4	FRONTISPIECE 5	COLUMN OR ENGAGED COLUMN 6	PIER OR PILASTER 7	DORIC CAPITAL 8	IONIC CAPITAL 9	CORINTHIAN CAPITAL 10	BUTTRESS 11	SPANDREL 12
QUOINS 13	TIE ROD 14	CORNER BOARD 15	HALF-TIMBERING 16	SKIRT-ROOF 17	CORBELLING 18	STRING OR BELT COURSE 19	PLINTH 20	ENTABLATURE 21	PLAIN PARAPET 22	CRENELLATED PARAPET 23	GABLED PARAPET 24
STEPPED PARAPET 25	DECORATED PARAPET 26	CARVING 27	PAINTED DESIGN 28	INSCRIPTION OR DATE STONE 29	DECORATIVE SHINGLE 30	DECORATIVE BRICK 31	DECORATIVE TILE OR TERRA COTTA 32	BALCONY 33	BALCONET 34	UPPER STOREY DOOR 35	OVERHANG 36
OTHER 37											

32 ROOF TYPE

LOW GABLE 01	MEDIUM GABLE 02	HIGH GABLE 03	HIPPED GABLE 04	GABLE-FLAT 05	PYRAMIDAL 06	LOW HIP 07	MEDIUM HIP 08	HIGH HIP 09	GABLED HIP 10	GAMBREL 11	HIPPED GAMBREL 12
MANSARD, 4 SIDES 13	MANSARD, 2 SIDES 14	MANSARD, 1 SIDE 15	GAMBREL, 1 SIDE 16	SHED 17	SALTBOX 18	FLAT 19	SAWTOOTH 20	MONITOR 21	DOMED 22	CONICAL 23	VAULTED OR ARCHED 24
BUTTERFLY 25	POLYGONAL 26	OTHER 27									

33 ROOF TYPE – SPECIAL SHAPES (MULTIPLE CHOICE)

NONE	CENTRE GABLE (FACADE)	OFFSET GABLE (FACADE)	CROSS GABLE	DOUBLE GABLE (FACADE)	MORE THAN TWO GABLES (FACADE)	ADDITIONAL GABLE (NOT ON FACADE)	TRUNCATED, ANY ROOF TYPE	BELLCAST, ANY ROOF TYPE	OTHER		
1	2	3	4	5	6	7	8	9	10		

34 ROOF SURFACE MATERIAL

UNKNOWN	THATCH OR SOD	WOOD	SLATE	ASPHALT SHINGLE	TILE OR TERRA COTTA	TAR AND GRAVEL	CONCRETE	METAL	GLASS	OTHER
01	02	03	04	05	06	07	08	09	10	11

35 ROOF TRIM – EAVES (MULTIPLE CHOICE)

NOT APPLICABLE	FLUSH EAVES	PROJECTING EAVES	RAFTERS EXPOSED	PLAIN FASCIA	MOULDED FASCIA	DECORATED FASCIA	PLAIN SOFFIT	MOULDED SOFFIT	DECORATED SOFFIT	PLAIN FRIEZE	MOULDED FRIEZE
1	2	3	4	5	6	7	8	9	10	11	12
DECORATED FRIEZE 13	BRACKETS 14	CORBELLED CORNICE 15	OTHER 16								

36 ROOF TRIM MATERIAL – EAVES

NONE	UNKNOWN	WOOD	STONE	BRICK	PLASTER OR STUCCO	TILE OR TERRA COTTA	CONCRETE	METAL	OTHER
01	02	03	04	05	06	07	08	09	10

37 ROOF TRIM – VERGES (MULTIPLE CHOICE)

NOT APPLICABLE	FLUSH VERGES	PROJECTING VERGES	PURLINS EXPOSED	PLAIN FASCIA	MOULDED FASCIA	DECORATED FASCIA	PLAIN SOFFIT	MOULDED SOFFIT	DECORATED SOFFIT	PLAIN FRIEZE	MOULDED FRIEZE
1	2	3	4	5	6	7	8	9	10	11	12
DECORATED FRIEZE 13	BRACKETS 14	CORBELLED CORNICE 15	RETURNED EAVES 16	PEDIMENT 17	OTHER 18						

38 ROOF TRIM MATERIAL – VERGES

NONE	UNKNOWN	WOOD	STONE	BRICK	PLASTER OR STUCCO	TILE OR TERRA COTTA	CONCRETE	METAL	OTHER
01	02	03	04	05	06	07	08	09	10

CA: Sample page from *Selection Form.*

INVENTAIRE GÉNÉRAL DES MONUMENTS
ET RICHESSES ARTISTIQUES DE LA FRANCE

- Ecrire en majuscules les noms propres

- Entourer les descripteurs préimprimés pertinents

- Dans le cas d'une réponse multiple, séparer les descripteurs par des tirets. Ne pas employer le tiret (ou trait d'union) dans les descripteurs eux-mêmes.

BORDEREAU ARCHITECTURE

1000 |—_____|
(n° machine)

5 |— DOSSIER| |— PHOTOGRAMMÉTRIE| |— THÉODOLITE|

|—_____| |—_____|
(n° microfiche texte)   (n° microfiche photo)

1010 |—_____|
(Dénomination)

1030 |—_____|
(Genre du destinataire)

10 |—_____|
(Titres - Appellations - Précisions sur la dénomination)

|—_____|
(Destination actuelle précédée d'actuellement)

1060 |—_____|
(Parties constituantes)

|_____|

1070 |—_____|
(Représentation)

|_____|

20 |—_____|
(Précisions concernant la représentation)

|_____|

|_____|

1130 |—_____| |—_____|
(Région)   (n° dept)

|—_____| |—_____|
(Canton)   (Commune)

30 |—_____|
(Lieu-dit ou secteur urbain)

40 |—_____|
(Adresse et / ou numérotation artificielle)

151

FR: Original form.

1140 |— ŒUVRE NON REPÉRÉE | |— |
(Pour un édifice) (Musée pour un édicule et parties déplacées)

|— ŒUVRE DISPARUE | |— COMMUNICATION DE L'ADRESSE INTERDITE |
(Pour un édicule)

50 |— CAD.

|—
(Pour un édicule ou parties déplacées, édifice de conservation non inventorié)

OU

50 |— |—
(Dénomination de l'édifice de conservation) (Son destinataire)

|— |—
(Son titre) (L'emplacement précis)

1170 |— LAMBERT |— X = ( ) |— Y = ( )
(n° zone Lambert)

|— XO = ( ) |— XE = ( )

|— YN = ( ) |— YS = ( )

1210 |— EN AGGLOMÉRATION | |— EN VILLE | |— EN VILLAGE | |— EN ÉCART | |— ISOLÉ |

1250 |— REMPLOIS | |— REMPLOIS PROVENANT DE | |— PROVENANT DE |

|— |—
(Etat ou n° dépt) (Canton)

|—
(Commune)

1260 |— PARTIES DÉPLACÉES | |— PARTIES DÉPLACÉES A |

|— |—
(Etat ou n° dépt) (Canton)

|—
(Commune)

1310 |—
(Auteurs)

|—

|—

1320 |— SIGNATURE | |— ATTRIBUTION AVEC RÉFÉRENCE |

|— ATTRIBUTION PAR SOURCE | |— ATTRIBUTION PAR TRAVAUX HISTORIQUES |

1370 |— _____ |
(Epoque ou siècle)

|_____|

|_____|

|_____|

|— ANNÉE (_____) | |— PORTE LA DATE|

|— DATE AVEC RÉFÉRENCE| |— DATE PAR SOURCE| |— DATE PAR TRAVAUX HISTORIQUES|

60 |— _____ |
(Historique)

|_____|

|_____|

|_____|

|_____|

|_____|

|_____|

|_____|

|_____|

1390 |— _____ |
(Matériau du gros œuvre)

|_____|

1400 |— _____ |
(Matériau de couverture)

1410 |— ÉTUDIÉ (_____)| |— REPÉRÉ (_____)| |— BATI (_____)|
(Pour un bordereau collectif)

1420 |— _____ |
(Parti de plan)

1430 |— _____ |
(Vaisseaux et étages)

1450 |— _____ |
(Technique de décor)

1460 |— ÉLÉVATION A TRAVÉES | |— ÉLÉVATION ORDONNANCÉE |

|— ÉLÉVATION ORDONNANCÉE SANS TRAVÉES |

1470 |—
(Type de couverture)

1480 |—
(Type de couvrement)

1490 |— H. (   ) | |— LONG. (   ) | |— LARG. (   ) | |— PROF. (   ) |
(Pour un édicule , dimensions en cm)

1500 |—
(Emplacement et forme des escaliers)

70 |—
(Typologie régionale)

1510 |— DÉTRUIT | |— DÉTRUIT APRES INVENTAIRE |

|— VESTIGES | |— MAUVAIS ÉTAT | |— MENACÉ | |— RESTAURÉ |

1550 |— PROPRIÉTÉ PUBLIQUE | |— PROPRIÉTÉ DE L'ETAT |

|— PROPRIÉTÉ PRIVÉE | |— PROPRIÉTÉ DU DÉPARTEMENT |

|— PROPRIÉTÉ PRIVÉE PERSONNE MORALE | |— PROPRIÉTÉ DE LA COMMUNE |

|—
(Protection M. H. avec la date en affixe)

|—
(Dépôt pour les édicules et parties déplacées)

1590 |— A SIGNALER |

80 |—
(Mise à jour de la microfiche)

154

MINISTÈRE DE LA CULTURE ET DE LA COMMUNICATION

DIRECTION DU PATRIMOINE

INDICATEUR DU PATRIMOINE
(Architecture)

Département de l'Eure

ARRONDISSEMENT
DES
ANDELYS

INVENTAIRE GÉNÉRAL

DES MONUMENTS ET DES RICHESSES ARTISTIQUES DE LA FRANCE

RÉPERTOIRE

DES OEUVRES ÉTUDIÉES

ALIZAY

10— MAISONS; FERMES. ETUDIE(1); REPERE(11); BATI(291). [LAMBERT1; XO=(51438); XE=(51715); YN=(18330); YS=(17885)] 17E SIECLE; 18E SIECLE; 19E SIECLE. GRANGE; ETABLE. CALCAIRE; BRIQUE; BOIS; PAN DE BOIS; MOELLON. TUILE PLATE; ARDOISE. 1185; 743A8.

ALIZAY

11— EGLISE PAROISSIALE. SAINT GERMAIN. [CAD. 1978 B1 64 LAMBERT1; X=(51554); Y=(18071)] VESTIGES DE L EDIFICE DU 12E SIECLE DANS LE MUR SUD DU CHOEUR; FENETRE DU 14E SIECLE SUR LE CHEVET; BRAS DU TRANSEPT. TOUR CLOCHER ET CULOTS SCULPTES 16E SIECLE; NEF REFAITE AU 18E SIECLE. FACADE OCCIDENTALE 4E QUART 19E SIECLE; PATRONAGE: L ARCHEVEQUE DE ROUEN(76) PROPRIETE DE LA COMMUNE ENCLOS; CIMETIERE CALCAIRE; MOELLON; PIERRE DE TAILLE ARDOISE. 1189; 743A10.

12— MAISON. RUE DE L ANDELLE [CAD. 1974 C3 426 LAMBERT; X=(51583); Y=(18073)] MILIEU 19E SIECLE. PROPRIETE PRIVEE BRIQUE; REVETEMENT ARDOISE 1186; 743B12.

\# **13— CHATEAU FORT.** OEUVRE NON REPERE [LAMBERT1; XO=(51438); XE=(51715); YN=(18330); YS=(17885)] 11E SIECLE ? DETRUIT MOTTE. 1188; 743B14.

ROUVILLE

\# **14— CHATEAU.** [CAD. 1973 C2 167 A 170. LAMBERT1; XO=(51580); XE=(51620); YN=(18035); YS=(17990)] CHEMINEE 1ERE MOITIE 17E SIECLE. VESTIGE DE L EDIFICE ANTERIEUR; COLOMBIER 18E SIECLE; CHATEAU ET COMMUNS RECONSTRUITS EN 1882 PAR LOISEL. ARCHITECTE A ROUEN; CHAPELLES SAINT PIERRE ET SAINT ANTOINE DETRUITES MAUVAIS ETAT PROPRIETE PRIVEE PERSONNE MORALE PARTIES AGRICOLES; COMMUNS; ECURIES; PORTAIL; COLOMBIER; GRANGE; PARC; CHEMINEE; CHAPELLE CALCAIRE; PIERRE DE TAILLE; MOELLON. ARDOISE. 1187; 743C1.

- 4 -

TYPOLOGIE-INDEX

CELLIER LISORS. 755. PONT DE L ARCHE. 1002. RADEPONT. 1065. [3].

CHAPELLE ALIZAY 14 ANDELYS(LES) 37 \# 58 83 AUBEVOYE 108 \# 109 112 \# BACQUEVILLE. 137 BAZINCOURT SUR EPTE. 145 BEAUFICEL EN LYONS. 151 153 BEZU LA FORET 174 178 \# BEZU SAINT ELOI 185 BOURG BEAUDOIN 233 BUS SAINT REMY. 240 CHARLEVAL 268 \# 269 \# 271 CHAUVINCOURT PROVEMONT 207 COUDRAY EN VEXIN 226 CRIQUEBEUF SUR SEINE 227 \# CROIX SAINT LEU

CHATEAU AILLY 4 ALIZAY 14 AMECOURT 18 AMFREVILLE SOUS LES MONTS 29 ANDELYS(LES) 78 \# 80 95 AUBEVOYE 111 AUTHEUIL AUTHOUILLET 116 AUTHEVERNES 128 BAZINCOURT SUR EPTE. 145 BERNOUVILLE 160 BERTHENONVILLE 166 BEZU LA FORET 174 BOIS JEROME SAINT OUEN 190

CHATEAU FORT ALIZAY 13 \# ANDELYS(LES) 76 BACQUEVILLE 140 \# BAZINCOURT SUR EPTE 143 144 BEZU SAINT ELOI 184 BOIS JEROME SAINT OUEN 191 BUS SAINT REMY 240 CHARLEVAL 284 \# CHATEAU SUR EPTE 226 DOUVILLE SUR ANDELLE 297 ETREPAGNY 443 GAILLON 558 GAMACHES EN

CHEMINEE ALIZAY 14 AMFREVILLE SOUS LES MONTS 33 ANDELYS(LES) 51 \# BUS SAINT REMY. 236 CHARLEVAL. 271. 272. MEZIERES EN VEXIN 865. [7].

CIMETIERE ALIZAY 11 AMECOURT 16 AMFREVILLE SOUS LES MONTS 31 AUTHEVERNES 125 BERNOUVILLE 158 BOUAFLES 217 BOUCHEVILLIERS 225 BOURG BEAUDOIN 229 BUS SAINT REMY 238

- 105 -

FR: Composite sample from *Indicateur du patrimoine architectural, arrondissement des Andelys,* published directly from computerized data.

MATERIAUX-INDEX

APPAREIL MIXTE AMECOURT 16 AMFREVILLE SOUS LES MONTS 28 31 ANDELYS(LES) 63 AUTHEUIL AUTHOUILLET 119 BACQUEVILLE 130 131 BAZINCOURT SUR EPTE 142 BEAUFICEL EN LYONS 149.

ARDOISE AILLY 3 4 ALIZAY 11 12 14 AMECOURT 16 17 18 AMFREVILLE LES CHAMPS 22 23 24 AMFREVILLE SOUS LES MONTS 28 29 30 31 33 ANDELYS(LES) 40 45 48 55 58 66 84 AUBE-

BOIS AILLY 2 6 7 9 ALIZAY 10 AMECOURT 19 AMFREVILLE LES CHAMPS 21 25 AMFREVILLE SOUS LES MONTS 27 34 ANDELYS(LES) 45 50 51 # 58 59 60 62 64 65 67 70 81 83 88 91

- 119 -

CHRONOLOGIE-INDEX

DEBUT 4E QUART 17E SIECLE RENNEVILLE 1070 THILLIERS EN VEXIN(LES) 1200 #. [2].

FIN 4E QUART 17E SIECLE AUTHEUIL AUTHOUILLET 119 BEZU LA FORET 178 # PITRES 963 SAINTE BARBE SUR GAILLON 1158 VESLY 1323. [5].

LIMITE 17E SIECLE 18E SIECLE DOUDEAUVILLE EN VEXIN 390 GAILLON 558. [2].

18E SIECLE AILLY 2 ALIZAY 10 11 14 AMECOURT 16 19 AMFREVILLE LES CHAMPS 21 24 AM-FREVILLE SOUS LES MONTS 27 34 ANDELYS(LES) 50 58 63 64 67 68 71 74 77 88 91 95 97 AU-

- 127 -

AUTEURS-INDEX

LEQUESNE HOUVILLE EN VEXIN 711. [1].

LOISEL ALIZAY 14. [1].

LOURME(MATHURIN DE) GISORS 583. [1].

MAILLET DU BOULLAY VAUDREUIL(LE) 1311. [1].

- 136 -

OEUVRES A SIGNALER OU DETRUITES

CLASSE M. H. AMFREVILLE SOUS LES MONTS 33 ANDELYS(LES) 40 55 58 76 87 AUTHEUIL AU-

INSCRIT M. H. AILLY 3 ANDELYS(LES) 39 45 AUBEVOYE 100 101 AUTHEVERNES 127 BEAUFICEL

SITE CLASSE AMFREVILLE SOUS LES MONTS 28 BEAUFICEL EN LYONS 149. BERTHENONVILLE 165

SITE INSCRIT AMFREVILLE LES CHAMPS 22 BAZINCOURT SUR EPTE 142 BERNOUVILLE 158 CHA-

AUTRES OEUVRES A SIGNALER AILLY 9 ALIZAY 14 AMECOURT 16 19 AMFREVILLE LES CHAMPS 23 25 AMFREVILLE SOUS LES MONTS 29 ANDELYS(LES) 36 51 # 52 61 68 73 79 83 84 88 91

OEUVRE DETRUITE ALIZAY 13 # AMFREVILLE LES CHAMPS 26 # ANDELYS(LES) 37 # 41 # 43

- 141 -

TOPONYMES-INDEX

ROULE(LE) AUBEVOYE 108 # ROSAY SUR LIEURE 1106. [2].

ROUVILLE ALIZAY 14 HEBECOURT 663. [2].

SABLONS(LES) IGOVILLE 726. [1].

- 151 -

Echelle : 1/100.000°

Limite d'arrondissement

Les coordonnées Lambert 1 (Zone Nord) ont été simplifiées par la suppression du chiffre des centaines de kilomètres qui apparaît néanmoins dans l'angle S.O. de la carte.
Chaque carré du carroyage est désigné par les coordonnées de son angle S.O.

© IGN.

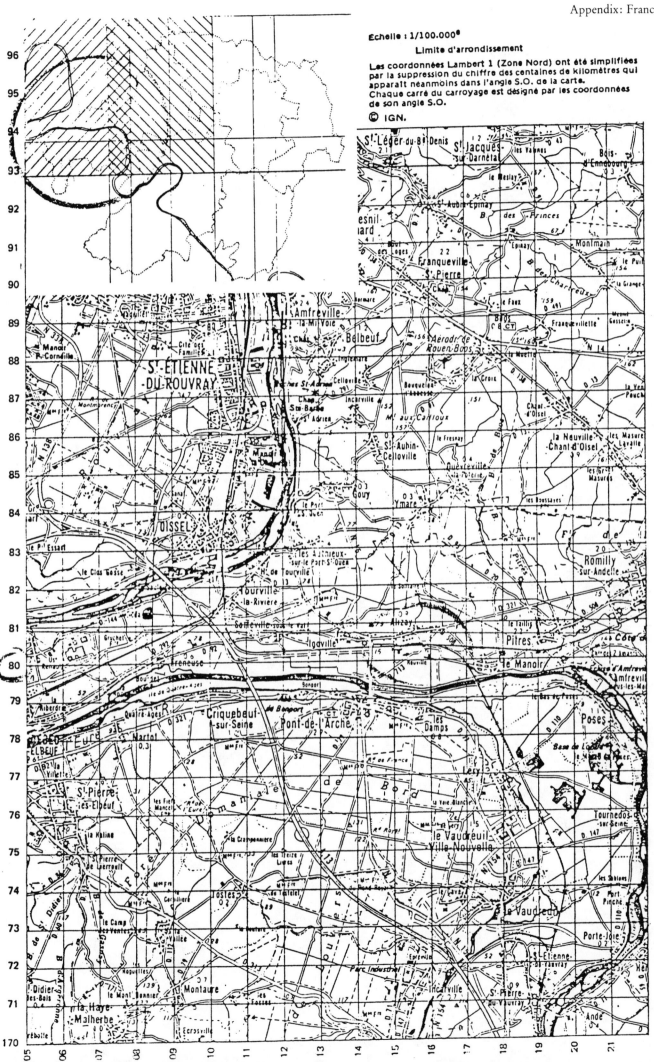

ARCHAEOLOGICAL SURVEY OF INDIA

FORM A

RECORD OF PROTECTED MONUMENTS AND SITES

(to be filled in duplicate by Circle Offices for all protected monuments and sites and one copy with enclosures to be sent to the Director General)

STATE

District

1. Name of monument/site as given in the Notification (also alternative names, if any)

2. Locality

3. Lat.   N.   Long.   E.   1" Survey sheet No.

4. Sub-division   Tehsil/Taluk

   Revenue Circle   Police Station

   Post Office

5. Approach (including nearest railway station, transport and halting facilities and authority to be addressed for reservation of accommodation)

6. Brief history, importance and outstanding features of the monument, including reference to sculptures, paintings, inscriptions, etc. (*Selected photographs and, if possible, sketches to be pasted on sheets to be attached*)

GIPN—S7—5 Dir. of Arch./61—6-4-63—5,000.

IN1:   Original form.

7

COPIES OF NOTIFICATIONS

(If the Notifications relate to more than one monument or site, relevant extracts should be given)

2

6. *(Contd.)*

7. Published references (selected but including references to Imperial and District Gazetteers and local Manuals)

8. Topographical features

9. Climatic data (temperature, rainfall, etc.)

10. Authority, nos. and dates of notifications:

    (i) preliminary

    (ii) confirmatory

    (copies to be typed on pp. 7-8)

21. Staff attached to the monument/site

22. References to photographs in the office (selected)

23. References to drawings in the office (selected)

24. Any other remarks

25. Signature of the Superintendent and date

FORM A (*contd.*)

4

11. Section and Act under which protected

12. Ownership. If Government, whether it was received as a gift or bequest; *if so, quote Section and Act and attach copy of instrument*

13. Whether any agreement with the owner exists; *if so, quote Section and Act and type copy of agreement on pp. 9-12*

14. Utilization, if any, under agreement or otherwise

15. Any revenue from endowment, lease, etc.

16. Area and boundary according to Notification/other official and revenue records/ convention. (*Strike out term not applicable*)

17. Recorded classification, if any

5

18. References to office-files containing important inspection, conservation (including chemical), epigraphical and horticultural notes, administrative matters, etc.

19. Brief note on outstanding structural and chemical conservation so far carried out

20. Nature and extent of garden, if any, attached to the monument

Ledger of Historic Sites, Places of Scenic Beauty
and/or Natural Monuments

史 跡 名 勝 天 然 記 念 物 台 帳

Kind 種別		Name 名 称		Designation 指定	Date 年 月 日（ 年 月 日官報告示第 号）
					年 月 日（ 年 月 日官報告示第 号）
Location 所在地				Alteration 異動	Date and number of announcement in the official gazette
				管理者—Custodian	

指定 の 理由 Causes of Designation

イ 史跡名勝天然記念物指定基準

　　　　　　　　　　　の部第　　By par. _____, item _____ of criteria for Designation
of Historic Sites, Places of Scenic Beauty and/or
Natural Monuments

ロ 説明 Explanation

文 化 財 保 護 委 員 会

Commission for Protection of
Cultural Property
(Now Agency for Cultural Affairs)

Requisites for conservation

保存の

要 件

Documents

資 料

報 告 書 第 No. _____ of Reports on _____

写真 枚（写真台帳 ）・土地台帳附属地図 枚・実測図 枚・拓本 枚

_____ sheets of photographs   _____ sheets of   _____ sheets of   _____ sheets of
                                              maps attached to   drawings   engraved prints
(No. _____ of the Photograph Ledger)   the terrier

JP2: Original form.

Items Concerning Designated Area and Others
指定地域等に関する事項

総地積 Total area of lands	総筆数 Total number of lots	国有地 Land in government possession	筆数 Number of lots	地積 Acreage	民有地 Land in private possession	筆数 Number of lots	地積 Acreage

郡市区 District·City Ward	町村 Town·Village	大字 Major section	字 Minor section	地番 Lot number	地目 Land category	地積 Acreage	所有者・占有者の住所及び氏名又は名称 Name and address of owner and possessor	備考 Remarks

Commission for Protection
of Cultural Property
(Now Agency for Cultural Affairs)

文化財保護委員会

郡市区	町村	大字	字	地番	地目	地積	所有者・占有者の住所及び氏名又は名称	備考
					ditto			

CUESTIONARIO No. 1.

Conteste las siguientes preguntas

1. ¿Qué monumentos religiosos construídos en el periodo 1521 a 1900 existen en su parroquia?

LLENANDO ESTE CUADRO DIGANOS LOS MAYORES DETALLES DE CADA MONUMENTO

NOMBRE DE LA POBLACION Y DEL MUNICIPIO	ADVOCACION	FECHA APROXI-MADA	ORDEN MONASTICA ORIGINAL	FORMA DE ATRIO 1 2 3	CRUZ ATRIAL TIENE NO TIENE	NUMERO DE TORRES	TECHO DE LA NAVE PRINCIPAL	RETABLOS IMPORTAN-TES

2. ¿Se conservan en buen estado los archivos parroquiales? Díganos desde que época existen documentos.
3. ¿En que fechas se acostumbra en esa parroquia celebrar ferias y fiestas tradicionales?
4. ¿Qué leyendas y tradiciones religiosas o profanas existen en la parroquia a su cargo?
5. Mandar fotografías exteriores, interiores y planos sí es posible.

MX1:   Original form.

INSTITUTO NACIONAL DE ANTROPOLOGIA E HISTORIA
DEPARTAMENTO DE CATALOGO

NUM.	TIPO	NOMBRE MONUMENTO	SIGLO	LOCALIZACION	POBLACION	MUNICIPIO	EDO
0361	01	CASA	19	MOCTEZUMA 109	AGUASCALIENTES	007	AGS
0362	01	CASA	19	VENUSTIANO CARRANZA 229	AGUASCALIENTES	007	AGS
0363	01	CASA	19	VENUSTIANO CARRANZA 401	AGUASCALIENTES	007	AGS
0364	01	CASA	18	CONTRERAS 121	AGUASCALIENTES	007	AGS
0365	01	CASA	18	CONTRERAS 127 Y 114	AGUASCALIENTES	007	AGS
0366	01	CASA	19	ZETINA 116 Y 123	AGUASCALIENTES	007	AGS
0367	01	CASA	19	MOCTEZUMA GUTIERREZ 320	AGUASCALIENTES	007	AGS
0368	01	CASA	18	RIVERO Y VERDAD 114	AGUASCALIENTES	007	AGS
0369	01	CASA	19	PRIMO VERDAD TORO 215	AGUASCALIENTES	007	AGS
0371	01	CASA	19	JUAN DE MONTORO 222	AGUASCALIENTES	007	AGS
0372	01	CASA	19	JUAN DE MONTORO 228	AGUASCALIENTES	007	AGS
0373	01	CASA Y COMERCIO	18	GUADALUPE 432	AGUASCALIENTES	007	AGS
0374	01	CASA Y COMERCIO	19	ALLENDE 309	AGUASCALIENTES	007	AGS
0375	01	PALACIO DE GOBIERNO	19	MORELOS 309	AGUASCALIENTES	007	AGS
0376	01	PALACIO MUNICIPAL	19	MORELOS 301	AGUASCALIENTES	007	AGS
0263	02	HOTEL FRANCIA COMERCIO	19	PLAZA PRINCIPAL SUR	AGUASCALIENTES	007	AGS
0264	02	OFICINAS Y COMERCIO	19	PLAZA PRINCIPAL SUR	AGUASCALIENTES	007	AGS
0265	02	HABITACION COMERCIO	19	JUAREZ MADERO 102	AGUASCALIENTES	007	AGS
0267	02	HABITAC COMER	18	PLAZA PRINCIPAL 127	AGUASCALIENTES	007	AGS
0268	02	HOTEL PARIS	19	PLAZA PRINCIPAL 121	AGUASCALIENTES	007	AGS
0269	02	HOTEL IMPERIAL	19	PLAZA PRINCIPAL	AGUASCALIENTES	007	AGS
0270	02	CASA DE LA CULTURA	18	MOCTEZUMA 101	AGUASCALIENTES	007	AGS
0271	02	OF FED DE SRIA DE S	18	VENUSTIANO CARRANZA 101	AGUASCALIENTES	007	AGS
0272	02	COLEGIO	18	VENUSTIANO CARRANZA 115	AGUASCALIENTES	007	AGS
0273	02	COLEGIO	19	VENUSTIANO CARRANZA 118	AGUASCALIENTES	007	AGS
0274	02	HOTEL REFORMA	19	MANUEL M PONCE 120	AGUASCALIENTES	007	AGS
0275	02	TEATRO MORELOS COMERCIO	18	NIETO 119	AGUASCALIENTES	007	AGS
0276	02	HABITACION COMERCIO	19	PLAZA DE LA REPUBLICA	AGUASCALIENTES	007	AGS
0277	02	HABITACION COMERCIO	19	MADERO Y JUAREZ 102	AGUASCALIENTES	007	AGS
0278	02	HABITACION COLECTIVA	19	5 DE MAYO 123	AGUASCALIENTES	007	AGS
0279	02	INST AUTONOMO CIENCI	18	MORELOS 221 A 129 JUAREZ 102	AGUASCALIENTES	007	AGS
0280	02		18	PALMIRA 101 A 129 COLON 126	AGUASCALIENTES	007	AGS
0281	02			JARDIN DEL ESTUDIANTE 3	AGUASCALIENTES	007	AGS
0282	02				AGUASCALIENTES	007	AGS

MX: Sample print-out from *Monumentos y Lugares de Belleza Natural.*

ROYAUME DU MAROC — INVENTAIRE DU PATRIMOINE CULTUREL

MONUMENT N°

cf. — Site N°

Province, chef — lieu :

Cercle :

Quartier, lieu–dit :

Situation exacte :

Ville, commune :

Dénomination :

Cadastre :

Propriétaire, adminis-tration responsable

Cadre et contenu :

Epoque de construction :

Utilisation actuelle :

Description :

Oeuvres d'art mobilières :

Etat actuel, observations :

Gros — œuvre

Parties com-plémentaires

Toiture

Intérieur

Degré de protection à appliquer

Conservation intégrale
Conservation partielle
Reconstruction possible

ascen-dante

Conden-sation

Plafond, terrasse

Etat de Conservation

Satisfaisant
Médiocre
Mauvais

Humidité

Nulle
Traces
Forte

Protection légale :

Enquête   N° :   Date :
Classement   N° :   Date :
Déclassement   N° :   Date :
Inscription   N° :   Date :

Rédigée par :   le
Contrôlée par :   le
Révisée par :   le

Nature de la décision

Documents graphiques et photographiques

Le recto de cette fiche constitue la fiche principale. Voir au verso la fiche complémentaire.

MA3:   Original form.

FICHE COMPLEMENTAIRE

MONUMENT N°

Données typologiques

Données chronologiques

Données techniques

Histoire et traditions populaires

Evolution subie :

Matériaux :

Utilisation proposée :

Opérations de restauration (en cours ou à l'étude) :

Caractéristiques particulières :

Utilisation possible :

Perspectives de restauration :

Bibliographie de base :

Visité par :   Date :

N° du dossier :

Observations, dangers éventuels :

Rédigée, par :   le :
Contrôlée par :   le :
Révisée par :   le :

Documentation graphique

Autres sources documentaires — Origine

études et rapports . . . .

Cartes. . . . .

Plans . . . .

Photographies . . . .

Diapositives. . . . .

Films . . . .

Autres archives . . . .

NEW YORK CITY LANDMARKS PRESERVATION COMMISSION
URBAN CULTURAL RESOURCES SURVEY FIELD FORM

Meredith Sykes, *Director of Survey* ©

Questions	UCRS Codes	Computer Fields (Inclusive)
1. Borough	1. _	1
2. Block No.	2. _ _ _ _ _	2-6
3. Lot No.	3. _ _ _ _	7-10
4. (If in Part)	4. _ _ _	11-13
5. Street	5. _ _ _ _ _	14-18
6. Numeric Address	6. _ _ _ _ _ _ _	19-25
7. (If non-numeric address)	7. _ _ _	26-28
8. (If also known as, street)	8. _ _ _ _ _	29-33
9. (If also known as, numeric)	9. _ _ _ _ _ _ _	34-40
10. Community	10. _ _ _ _	41-44
11. Film Roll No.	11. _ _ _ _	45-48
12. Film Shot, First	12. _ _	49-50
13. Film Shot, Last	13. _ _	51-52
14. Present Use, (1)	14. _ _ _ _	53-56
15. Present Use, (2)	15. _ _ _ _	57-60
16. Original Use, (1)	16. _ _ _ _	61-64
17. Original Use (2)	17. _ _ _ _	65-68
18. Style (1)	18. _ _	69-70
19. Style (2)	19. _ _	71-72
20. Style (3)	20. _ _	73-74
21. Significance	21. _ _	75-76
	Batch No. _ _ _	77-79
	Record No. <u>1</u>	80
	Geocode No. _ _ _ _ _ _	1-6
	_ _ _ _ _ _ _	7-13
22. Present Name	22. _ _ _ _ _ _	14-19
23. Original Name	23. _ _ _ _ _ _	20-25
24. Complex Name	24. _ _ _ _ _ _	26-31
25. Original Date	25. _ _ _	32-34
26. (If Estimated)	26. _	35
27. Date of Change	27. _ _ _	36-38
28. (If Estimated)	28. _	39

NYC: Original form.

29. Primary Architect(s) _____

_____ 29. _ _ _ _ _ _   40-45

30. (of Firm) _____ 30. _ _ _ _ _ _   46-51

31. Secondary Architect(s) _____

_____ 31. _ _ _ _ _ _   52-57

32. (of Firm) _____ 32. _ _ _ _ _ _   58-63

33. Massing of Structure _____ 33. _   64

Record No. <u>2</u>   80

Geocode No. _ _ _ _ _ _   1-6

_ _ _ _ _ _   7-13

34. (If, Number of Units in Structure) _____ 34. _ _   14-15

35. (If, Unit, Structure, Mirror Image, or Geocode) _____ 35. _   16
     1   2   3   4

36. Is Same as Street _____ 36. _ _ _ _ _   17-21

37. Is Same as Number _____ 37. _ _ _ _ _ _ _   22-28

38. Plot Width in Feet _____ 38. _ _ _ _   29-32

39. Plot Depth in Feet _____ 39. _ _ _ _   33-36

40. Building Width in Feet _____ 40. _ _ _ _   37-40

41. Building Depth in Feet _____ 41. _ _ _ _   41-44

42. Stories _____ 42. _ _ _   45-47

43. (If Basement) _____ 43. _   48

44. (If Attic) _____ 44. _   49

45. Bays _____ 45. _ _   50-51

Record No. <u>3</u>   80

Random Questions

	No.	Choice	Style	Material	Storey	
Geocode No.	_ _	_ _	_ _	_ _	_ _	1-13
_____	_ _	_ _	_ _	_ _	_ _	14-26
_____	_ _	_ _	_ _	_ _	_ _	27-39
_____	_ _	_ _	_ _	_ _	_ _	40-52
_____	_ _	_ _	_ _	_ _	_ _	53-65
_____	_ _	_ _	_ _	_ _	_ _	66-78

Record No. <u>4</u>   80

```
FILE: DEMO      NEW      TIME: 04/16/81 10:16:37    COMPUTER SERVICE CENTER


FOLLOWING IS SOME ENGLISH DATA PROVIDED BY MARKIV FOR THE
  MANHATTAN STREET ADDRESS: 31 CHAMBERS STREET.

  0000031 CHAMBERS STREET              MANHATTAN
  +
  COURTHOUSE, CITY OR COUNTY
  +
  BEAUX ARTS, FRENCH
  FREE CLASSIC
  +
  DESIG. EXT § INT LANDMARK ON NATIONAL REGISTER
  SURROGATES COURT
  HALL OF RECORDS
  +
  899
  THOMAS, JOHN R.
  +
  +
  HORGAN § SLATTERLY
  FACADE: STONE
  MANSARD ROOF
  ATTACHED FULLY SCULPTED FIGURATIVE SCULPTURE
  PEDIMENTAL DORMER ROOF
  PUBLIC INTERIOR SPACE
  BUILDING FEATURE: COLUMN OR PILASTER
  SINGLE STACK TALL DECORATED CHIMNEY


LINES WITH AN + SHOW NO DATA RECORDED FOR THAT QUESTION

ANY QUESTION OR COMBINATION OF QUESTIONS CAN BE USED FOR A MARKIV SORT.

FOR EXAMPLE, IF WE WISHED TO FIND SOME COURTHOUSES IN THE CITY LISTED
  ONLY BY BOROUGH, STREET ADDRESS, AND DATE THE FOLLOWING DATA WOULD
  BE COMPILED:

BOROUGH      ADDRESS        STREET    PRESENT USE                  DATE
BRONX        0000851 GRAND CONCOURSE  COURTHOUSE, CITY OR COUNTY   934
MANHATTAN    0000031 CHAMBERS STREET  COURTHOUSE, CITY OR COUNTY   899
MANHATTAN    0000026 FOLEY SQUARE     COURTHOUSE, FEDERAL OR STATE 933
RICHMOND     0000018 RICHMOND TERRACE COURTHOUSE, CITY OR COUNTY   922
RICHMOND     0000100 RICHMOND TERRACE COURTHOUSE, CITY OR COUNTY   930
```

NYC: Sample print-out.

OŚRODEK DOKUMENTACJI ZABYTKÓW W WARSZAWIE
KARTA EWIDENCYJNA ZABYTKÓW
ARCHITEKTURY I BUDOWNICTWA

A B C D E F G H I J K L Ł M N O P R S T U V W X Y Z | Nr

1. Obiekt

2. Czas powstania

3. Miejscowość

4. Adres

nr hipoteczny

5. Przynależność administracyjna

województwo

gmina

6. Poprzednie nazwy miejscowości

7. Przynależność administracyjna przed 1 VI 1975

województwo

powiat

8. Właściciel i jego adres

9. Użytkownik i jego adres

10. Rejestr zabytków

Nr .... data ....

11. Zdjęcia, plan sytuacyjny, rzuty

autor zdjęć
data wykonania
miejsce przechowywania negatywów

175

PL3: Original form.

13. Opis (sytuacja, materiał i konstrukcja, rzut, bryła, elewacja, dach, wnętrze wyposażenia, instalacje

12. Autorzy, historia obiektu, określenia stylu.

14. Kubatura

15. Powierzchnia użytkowa

16. Przeznaczenie pierwotne

17. Użytkowanie obecne

18. Prace budowlane i konserwatorskie, ich przebieg i dokumentacja

19. Stan zachowania (fundamenty, ściany zewnętrzne, ściany wewnętrzne, sklepienia, stropy, konstrukcje dachowe, pokrycie dachowe, pokrycie dachu, wyposażenie i instalacje)

20. Najpilniejsze postulaty konserwatorskie

21. Akta archiwalne (rodzaj akt, numer i miejsce przechowywania)

22. Bibliografia

23. Źródła ikonograficzne i fotografia (rodzaj, miejsce przechowywania, sygnatury)

24. Uwagi różne

25. Wypełnił

26. Sprawdził

27. Załączniki

Jed.Wyd. Akcyd. Olsztyn zam. 1603/S/75
Gatunek. ZP świecida. L.z. 1052 a. 20000

ODZ-wzór 1975r.

ZAMBIA SITE RECORD CARD: NATIONAL MONUMENTS COMMISSION

PROVINCE

SITE NAME

1   2 3 4 5 6 7 8 9 10 11 12 13 14 15 16 17 18 19 20 21

COORDINATES

22   23 ° 24   25   S

26   27 ° 28   29   E

CATEGORY

NATURAL/GEOLOGICAL/TRADITIONAL
ARCHAEOLOGICAL/HISTORICAL

SITE TYPE

32 33

STATUS

DECLARED/PROTECTED/CONFIRMED FINDSPOT

30   DESTROYED/UNCONFIRMED/   31

UNPROTECTED

34 35

PERIODS

MUSEUM OBJECTS

36 37 38 39 40

FILE REFS.

41   42 43   44 45 46   47 48 49   50

51

PUBLICATIONS

52

EXCAVATIONS

53

C.14 DATES

PROVINCE   SITE NAME   MAP

FARM/CHIEF/TOWN   ALTERNATE SITE NAMES

POSITION/DIRECTIONS

DESCRIPTION OF SITE

FINDS

OTHER INFORMATION

SOURCE/INFORMANT

ZM: Original form.

ZAMBIA NATIONAL MONUMENTS COMMISSION SITE INDEX

DATA CARDS CORRECTED TO JULY 1978

SITES OF ROCK PAINTINGS AND FINDS OF -

IRON AGE (INDETERMINATE)

SITE-NAME	PROV-INCE	COORDINATES	CATEGORY	STATUS	PERIODS	SITE-TYPE	MUSEUM OBJECTS	FILE-REFS
CHAYINGO HILL	EST	13-48S 32-15E	ARCHAEOLOG.	PROTECTED	IA+LSA OR IA	PNTD. CAVE+FINDS	9347	MC/016/66 + P
CHIKUNGU MISSION	EST		ARCHAEOLOG.	UNCONFIRMED	IA+LSA OR IA	PNTD. CAVE+FINDS	5728	
FIWILA MISSION	CNT	13-57S 29-37E	ARCHAEOLOG.	PROTECTED	LSA+IA	PNTD. CAVE+FINDS	6866	MC/016/55
KAMBULUMBULU ROCK SH	NTH	11-50S 32-55E	ARCHAEOLOG.	PROTECTED	LSA+IA	PNTD. CAVE+FINDS	9359	MC/021/120 + P EX
KAPIRI MPOSHI	CNT	13-53S 28-41E	ARCHAEOLOG.	PROTECTED	IA+LSA OR IA	PNTD. CAVE+FINDS	7081+	MON/604/69
MKOMA	EST	13-54S 32-12E	ARCHAEOLOG.	DECLARED	LSA+IA	PNTD. CAVE+FINDS	7291+	MC/016/66 + P
PETAMWIKA HILL	CPB	13-28S 28-44E	ARCHAEOLOG.	PROTECTED	LSA+IA	PNTD. CAVE+FINDS	9457+	
ROCKLANDS KATOLOA	EST	13-43S 32-39E	ARCHAEOLOG.	DECLARED	LSA+IA	PNTD. CAVE+FINDS	9342+	MUS/749/ + P EX
RUKUZYE E	EST	13-23S 32-52E	ARCHAEOLOG.	PROTECTED	IA+LSA OR IA	PNTD. CAVE+FINDS	9290	P
THANDWE	EST	13-40S 32-27E	ARCHAEOLOG.	DECLARED	LSA+IA	PNTD. CAVE+FINDS	8965+	P EX C14
WALAMBA	CPB	13-28S 28-42E	ARCHAEOLOG.	PROTECTED	IA+LSA OR IA	PNTD. CAVE+FINDS	9280	P
ZAWI HILL	EST	13-27S 32-48E	ARCHAEOLOG.	DECLARED	IA+LSA OR IA	PNTD. CAVE+FINDS	9340	MC/001/D02 + P

NATIONAL MONUMENTS

SITE-NAME	PROV-INCE	COORDINATES	CATEGORY	STATUS	PERIODS	SITE-TYPE	MUSEUM OBJECTS	FILE-REFS
MWELA ROCKS	NTH	10-10S 31-15E	ARCHAEOLOG.	DECLARED	LSA OR IA	PAINTED CAVE		MON/608/210+ P EX C14
MWELA ROCKS CAVE	NTH	10-10S 31-15E	ARCHAEOLOG.	DECLARED	LATER STONE A	CAVE+FINDS	7318	P EX C14
NACHIKUFU CAVES	NTH	12-07S 31-13E	ARCHAEOLOG.	DECLARED	LSA+EIA+LIA	PNTD. CAVE+FINDS	6299+	MC/049/46A + P
NACHITALO	CNT	13-30S 28-58E	ARCHAEOLOG.	DECLARED	LSA+LSA OR IA	PNTD. CAVE+FINDS		MUS/730
NDOLA SLAVE TREE	CPB	12-59S 28-37E	TRADITIONAL	DECLARED	TRADIT. ONLY	TRADITIONAL SITE		MC/014/222 + P
NIAMKOLO CHURCH	NTH	08-45S 31-08E	HISTORICAL	DECLARED	COLONIAL PER.	CHURCH/MISSION		MC/047/ + + P
NSALU	CNT	12-43S 30-40E	ARCHAEOLOG.	DECLARED	MSA+LSA+EIA+LI	PNTD CAVE+FINDS	6819+	MC/005 + P EX
NTEMBWE OF MWAZI LUN	EST	12-24S 33-22E	ARCHAEOLOG.	DECLARED	LATER IRON AGE	FORTIF. VILLAGE		MUS/746 EX
NTUMBACHUSI FALLS	LPL	09-52S 28-57E	NATURAL	DECLARED	NOT APPLICABLE	WATERFALL		MC/016/36 + P
NYAMBWEZU SHELTER	NWT	11-52S 25-05E	ARCHAEOLOG.	DECLARED	LSA OR IA	ENGRAVED CAVE	9002	MC/010/A98 + P

ZM: Sample print-out from *A classified Index of Archaeological and Other Sites in Zambia.*